DO WE NEED A MARRIAGE CONTRACT?

DO WE NEED A MARRIAGE CONTRACT?

Understanding How a Legal Agreement Can Strengthen Your Life Together

MICHAEL G. COCHRANE

B. A. LL. B.

John Wiley & Sons Canada, Ltd.

Library and Archives Canada Cataloguing in Publication Data

Cochrane, Michael G. (Michael George), 1953-
Do we need a marriage contract? : understanding how a legal agreement can strengthen your life together / Michael G. Cochrane.

Includes index.
ISBN 978-0-470-73751-4

1. Antenuptial contracts—Canada—Popular works. 2. Husband and wife—Canada—Popular works. I. Title.

KE559.C59 2010 346.7101'662 C2010-900204-0
KF529.C59 2010

Production Credits
Cover design: Adrian So
Interior text design and typesetter: Natalia Burobina
Cover photo: ©Getty Images/Brand X Pictures/Brian Haglwara
Printer: Printcrafters

John Wiley & Sons Canada, Ltd.
6045 Freemont Blvd.
Mississauga, Ontario
L5R 4J3

Printed in the Canada

1 2 3 4 5 PC 14 13 12 11 10

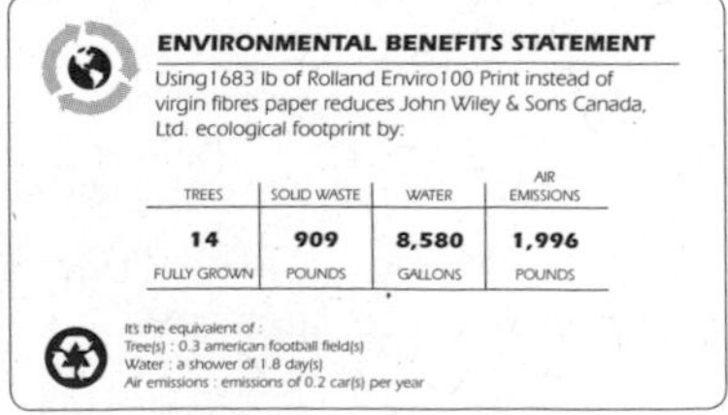

ENVIRONMENTAL BENEFITS STATEMENT

Using1683 lb of Rolland Enviro100 Print instead of virgin fibres paper reduces John Wiley & Sons Canada, Ltd. ecological footprint by:

TREES	SOLID WASTE	WATER	AIR EMISSIONS
14	**909**	**8,580**	**1,996**
FULLY GROWN	POUNDS	GALLONS	POUNDS

It's the equivalent of :
Tree(s) : 0.3 american football field(s)
Water : a shower of 1.8 day(s)
Air emissions : emissions of 0.2 car(s) per year

CONTENTS

ACKNOWLEDGEMENTS

I would like to acknowledge a few important people and their contribution to this book. I would like to acknowledge the combined forces of my literary agent, Daphne Hart, of Helen Heller agency (www.helenhelleragency.com) and my publisher, John Wiley & Sons Canada Ltd., who have worked with me as an author for this series of books about family law in Canada. This book, as well as *Surviving Your Divorce: A Guide to Canadian Family Law* and *Do You Need a Cohabitation Agreement?: Understanding How a Cohabitation Agreement Can Strengthen Your Life Together* is all about educating Canadians to be able to help themselves and to know when they need the help of professionals.

My assistant Lisa Henry deserves special mention as she is the one who helped me transform my scribbles into a manuscript over some very long days and nights.

Who we pick as our partners in life is critical to our happiness and I hope that as my daughters, Emma, Erica, Renée, and Hanna, head off into the world and form their important relationships they take some of my advice to heart. If any of them were about to marry, I would be sure to sit them down and hand them this book. Thanks too to my wife, Rita, who has shown great patience as I disappear for extended periods to do my writing. Thanks, Love.

Michael Cochrane
Partner, Ricketts, Harris LLP
181 University Avenue, Suite 816
Toronto, Ontario M5H 2X7

mcochrane@rickettsharris.com
www.rickettsharris.com
www.michaelcochrane.ca

CAUTION ABOUT LEGAL INFORMATION

The purpose of this book is to help Canadians who are married, getting married, or even thinking about it. I am providing legal information in this book, not legal advice. To obtain legal advice about the way that this information may apply to or affect your personal situation, I recommend that you speak with an experienced family law lawyer in your province or territory. This book is designed to make the conversation easier, less expensive, and more helpful.

1

IS THIS BOOK FOR YOU?

Canadians love to get married. Young, old, first time, second time, and even for the third time or more, we enter the bonds of matrimony full of optimism and hope. Some of those who get married may even know a little bit about the legal rights and responsibilities that are being created by their marriage. But for many (especially younger couples in first marriages), the experience is more about the wedding than about the marriage. The hall, the music, the photographer, the guest list, the cake, personalized vows, and even picking the song to which they will have their first dance consumes far more energy than their thinking about other important matters. Have they spent time thinking about a lifetime of joint financial planning, of raising children, of the possibility of injury or illness to one of them, of the impact of the marriage on their careers, property, and so on? Probably not. In some ways, it is understandable because the wedding is about celebrating love with family and friends. All that other stuff can seem like work and even scary. Possibility of death? Separation and divorce? Not interested.

Those challenges are the last things that we want to think about as we get married, yet they may be a part of your life together.

However, we need to remember something that is important—in Canada, most marriages work. We often hear people lamenting that 50% of marriages end in divorce, but this is not true. In Canada, the rate of divorce is closer to 38 percent. True, that is still high, but let's not forget that most marriages work. All marriages need help but it is those 38 percent of marriages that just don't make it that we need to worry about and which may be helped by marriage contracts.

In the next chapter, we are going to look at some tips that will certainly increase the likelihood of you having a successful marriage. But right now, let's consider whether you might need a marriage contract, or what are sometimes referred to as "prenups."

Let's start by considering a real case.

DIVORCE NIGHTMARE: DON'T LET THIS HAPPEN TO YOU

Gary and Sherry Leskun got married in 1978. Sherry was about 10 years older than Gary and she had been married before. She had two children from that marriage and was working at TD Bank when she met Gary. They hit it off and married, eventually having a daughter of their own. The three children were all blended into a happy family and Sherry kept working at the bank along with Gary. He, however, worked hard to improve his credentials, getting an MBA from the University of Western Ontario and becoming a certified general accountant. For them to pull this off financially, Sherry needed to cash in her RRSPs and even had TD Bank return her pension contributions.

Fifteen years into the marriage, in 1993, Gary left TD Bank and joined Motorola. A couple of years later, while Gary and Sherry were moving a generator at their home, she injured her back and needed surgery. The surgery did not go well and Sherry continued to suffer from back problems. Gary, on the other hand, was thriving at Motorola, and after five years, in 1998, they were so impressed that they moved him to Chicago to be their local Director of Program Development. Sherry, who had continued to work at the TD Bank, would join him in Chicago once he had settled. Unfortunately, while Gary was in Chicago, Sherry got some bad news that her position at TD was about to be eliminated. She applied for long-term disability benefits because of her ongoing back injury, and while the benefits were initially granted, they were discontinued a few years later.

Instead of having the opportunity to move to Chicago, Sherry was dealt another blow when Gary returned home five months later. He told her not to bother packing. He wanted a divorce. He had been having an affair for some time and wanted to marry the other woman, who lived in Chicago. You can imagine Sherry's reaction. Their legal case went all the way to the Supreme Court of Canada in what was described as the "scorched earth policy" of an embittered Sherry pursuing Gary in court to the point of obsession. She was so hurt by his misconduct and deceit in the marriage that she was unable to make a new life for herself. As one judge described it, "her life became the litigation." Sherry even represented herself in arguing the case before the Supreme Court of Canada.

Could Gary and Sherry have ever imagined that their life would evolve into a litigation nightmare? I don't think so. Would a marriage contract have helped them to avoid some of the painful issues that arose during their separation and divorce? I think a marriage contract could have helped them a great deal because they would have applied their minds to some of these issues, both before and while the marriage was under way.

Sherry was making financial sacrifices for Gary in good faith, hoping that it would benefit the family. Addressing that sacrifice by way of a marriage contract might have offered Sherry better financial security. By 2003, evidence before the court indicated that Gary, in his new life in Chicago, had a net worth of nearly a million dollars Canadian. Sherry, on the other hand, had received an $83,000 severance package from TD. She had received sole title to their townhouse and its contents, their RRSPs were equalized, a whole life insurance policy, their boat, and a loan that was outstanding (along with some credit cards) were divided equally. They agreed to retain their separate pensions and CPP credits as their sole property. Were they happy? No.

They had separated in 1998 and their case was finally dealt with by the Supreme Court of Canada in 2006, some eight years later—eight years of bitter and expensive litigation. It is my hope that some of the information in this book will help Canadians avoid situations like that suffered by the Leskuns.

Why Marriages Need Contracts

The possible need for a marriage contract may arise in three circumstances:

1. I am thinking about getting married, but have some concerns.

As each person approaches the possibility of marriage, there may be individual issues of concern. For example, one person may have received a substantial inheritance and wants to ensure that it remains protected in the marriage. Another person may have purchased a home before the marriage and wants to ensure that the initial investment is protected in the event of a separation. In some cases, families wish to provide their children with substantial wedding gifts of such things as down payments or actual homes. The parents worry that their gift may be lost if the marriage does not stand the test of time.

Consider the situation of a woman with two children who lives in Vancouver and is being asked to move to Toronto to marry for the second time. By marrying, she may jeopardize an entitlement to spousal support from her first marriage and divorce. In addition, she may have concerns about moving her children across the country without some specific understanding about how the children will be cared for in the new marriage. For example, what type of education will they receive in Toronto? In some cases, the couple entering the marriage may simply wish to have recognition of the assets that they bring into the relationship, left over from previous relationships that ended by divorce or death of a partner. Potential spouses in such situations could clearly benefit from a marriage contract that protects their interests.

As you can see, there are many reasons to consider the possibility of a marriage contract well in advance of the actual marriage.

2. I am married already but something has changed.

The need for a marriage contract may arise long after the marriage. Let's not forget that things change over time in our careers, in finances, and with the arrival of children. Consider the situation in which Lisa and Tom found themselves. They have been married for 10 years and have two children. Tom is a successful chartered accountant and is being offered a partnership with his firm. However, his potential partners have asked that Tom and Lisa sign a marriage contract in which she releases any interest she might have in Tom's partnership interests should they later separate. Tom's potential partners will ask for this type of marriage contract so that a subsequent divorce will not drag the partnership itself into litigation. Tom and Lisa's marriage has worked well, but why would Lisa sign such a marriage contract and give up an interest in this asset? A marriage contract in this situation would be of assistance because, in it, Tom and Lisa could agree that she would release her interest in Tom's partnership, but Tom would release any interest in the matrimonial home to compensate Lisa. This allows the marriage to continue to be strong, it allows Tom to pursue his business interest, which will benefit the family, and it protects Lisa by providing financial security.

The fact that a couple is already married does not mean that they may not find a use for a marriage contract as things change during the course of the marriage.

3. *I am thinking about getting separated.*

I know what you are thinking. Separated? Why would I need a marriage contract to separate? Sometimes a marriage gets into trouble, mistakes were made, and a decision is then made to end the marriage. In the middle of trying to unravel their marriage and related rights and responsibilities, one or both of the spouses may say something that suggests there is a glimmer of hope, "I wish he hadn't been so reckless with our finances. You know, other than that, he was a pretty good husband," or "I wish she had told me about her gambling. I could have found her help. Other than that, she was a pretty good wife."

Hearing these kinds of comments, a lawyer sometimes will pose questions to the client. What if we could solve that problem? Would you want to stay in the marriage? What if we designed a framework to ensure that problem is dealt with? What if we could protect you financially so that you can work on the relationship and not worry? At that point, a marriage contract may offer a solution to the problem that undermined the marriage. The couple stays married but with a new set of rules and protections.

As you can see, whether a person is planning to marry, already married, or experiencing trouble in their marriage, a marriage contract may have a lot to offer in strengthening the relationship.

TERMINOLOGY

Before we turn to a consideration of your actual relationship, let's consider some terminology. Confusion has arisen between the use of the terms "prenuptial agreement" and "marriage contract." Every prenuptial agreement is a marriage contract, but not every marriage contract is a prenuptial agreement. Prenuptial agreements are signed *before* the marriage, hence the "pre" in prenuptial. Once a couple is married, any agreement into which they enter dealing with their rights and responsibilities while married or upon separation or upon death, is called a marriage contract. For ease of reference, I will always refer to the contract as a marriage contract, whether it is signed before or after the wedding.

Let's turn now to doing some due diligence on the person you are about to marry—or to whom you have already made the big commitment of marriage.

2

EYES WIDE OPEN: DUE DILIGENCE AND RELATIONSHIP BUILDING

Before we examine the "legal parts" of marriage, let's look at the "people parts." You are making an important decision when you commit to marrying someone. Do you really know the person with whom you are about to share your life?

WHY DUE DILIGENCE?

If you were starting a new business with a partner or buying a business from someone, you would do what business people refer to as "due diligence." You would check out the potential partner. You would investigate thoroughly the books of the business that you are going to buy. You would make sure your money and your future are safe. The same approach should apply to relationships: make sure your future is safe. What should you be looking for? There are three areas of potential concern: health, criminal activity, and financial problems. Let's take a look at each of them.

Your Partner's Health

When we think of a person's health we tend to think of physical injuries, illness, or diseases. Those kinds of challenges are common for all of us. However, mental health issues can be just as daunting for couples and families. In this section I want to look at some of the key considerations as you do due diligence with respect to both types of health. Let's start with "physical."

Physical Health

Poor health can be hard on a relationship. Ask yourself honestly if you are prepared to stay in a relationship with someone who would require your care and support for a serious health challenge. Are you prepared to be in a relationship when you perhaps will carry the entire financial burden because your partner is too ill to work? I know this sounds harsh, but I have seen these types of challenges undermine a relationship very quickly. Disease, injury, illness—are any of these a factor in your partner's life? Any evidence that they may play a role in his or her family's life? Are there illnesses that your children might inherit given your partner's family history? Have you been open with your partner about disclosing your potential health challenges? What if your partner reveals to you that she or he has AIDS, multiple sclerosis, lupus, cancer, or any one of a number of devastating diseases? What would your decision about living together be if you learned that your partner's family has been devastated by breast cancer, or that your partner's family has a long history of alcoholism?

I'm not suggesting that this information should automatically result in an end to the relationship, but knowing about it before you commit to the relationship allows you to go into it with your eyes wide open. If and when these health challenges emerge, at least you knew what you might be in for in the relationship. Bottom line: learn about your partner's health and your partner's family's health, and answer honestly and completely the questions that are asked of you about your health and that of your family. Put it all on the table so that you both go into the relationship with your eyes wide open.

Mental Health

This type of health challenge is even more difficult. Here is an example of a real-life shocker that I encountered: a young couple began living together and everything was great for the first few years. Suddenly, she began to behave a little out of character. She went on wild shopping sprees to the United States and had casual sexual relations with strangers. She developed financial problems. She became depressed. She went through mood swings, and suddenly there were violent episodes. Her partner was in shock—what was happening to their relationship? The answer: she had stopped taking her antidepressant medication. He had no idea that she had been taking medication because she had kept her illness a secret. Was that fair to him? I don't think so. As a result, he was unwilling to work with her to restore some stability to her life and the relationship ended.

In the relationships that lawyers see going sour, mental health issues often loom large. I was involved in a case in which one partner suffered from obsessive compulsive disorder (OCD), which meant that, for her, non-stop cleaning of their home was absolutely necessary. The extent of her problem was not obvious until they were living together for several months, but gradually it became worse and worse. He noticed when he came home from work that their home now reeked of bleach. Suddenly, newspapers were forbidden in the house because they contained "germs." Similarly, no shoes were allowed in the house, and then *no people* were allowed in the house. Furniture was covered and they ate in the basement. Her OCD was out of control.

Would you want to know your partner suffered from that disorder before you started living together? Probably. What if your partner has schizophrenia, or suffers from manic depression? Wouldn't you want to know about it before you moved in? Me too. Bottom line: learn about your partner's mental health and their family's mental health background. Is there a history of depression in the family? Have there been suicides? These are valuable pieces of information that can help you understand what kind of relationship you may end up having with your partner. Both of you should put it all on the table and go into the relationship with your eyes wide open about any potential mental health challenges that may be down the road.

Criminal Problems

Knowing about your partner's past criminal activities or convictions is absolutely critical. In one situation that I encountered, a couple who had been married for several years and had two children set off on the children's dream trip to Florida and Disney World. For months the husband had resisted the trip. He had many excuses—too much work, not feeling well enough to make the trip. But he finally gave in after the children and their mother insisted that this particular March break, they were going to Disney World—no excuses. At the border they were stopped and, after having their passports and ID checked, were told to turn their car around and head back home. They were not granted access to the United States. Why? The husband had multiple convictions for fraud and a narcotics conviction to boot. He had simply been avoiding the border because he knew that his convictions could block access to the United States. The wife had no idea. It was his little secret about his past, a secret of which he was ashamed and had kept from her. She also now understood why he had turned down that great job offer that would have meant travel to the United States from time to time. How do you think she felt? What else had he kept secret? The marriage suffered.

What kinds of criminal activity have been discovered by couples after they were married? Consider the following situations other couples faced:

- His love of bicycling was not really related to his desire to help the environment but was simply because he had lost his licence after a conviction for impaired driving. His employment prospects were very limited geographically.
- She had been fired from a company and convicted of fraud for falsifying invoices and defrauding the business of thousands of dollars. She could never get hired for anything but casual jobs.
- He had several criminal charges and one conviction for assault against a previous wife. He could not travel to the United States.
- She had an accident in which someone was seriously injured while she drove without insurance. Her licence had been suspended for impaired driving. Now she was unable to get car insurance and the lawsuit had bankrupted her.

- He stole a friend's credit card and was convicted of fraud.
- She wrote bad cheques to a landlord.
- He had a gambling problem and a conviction for carrying a concealed weapon.
- She had a conviction for criminal harassment because she had stalked an old boyfriend and damaged his car by flattening all the tires.

Shall I go on? Wouldn't you rather know about these things before you start making commitments to each other? Bottom line: have a frank discussion with your partner and learn about his or her past and specifically about any problems your partner has had with the law.

Financial Problems

This is a big one. What do you really know about your partner's financial past, his or her earning capabilities, and ability to manage money? Over the years I have encountered couples who work as a team on their financial situation. They share information, invest together, and prosper together. However, I have also seen some spectacular financial screw-ups that have devastated couples. Why? Because one of them operated in a "secret financial world." Consider the following true stories. How would you feel in these situations?

- A couple's jointly-held home is now in jeopardy because she hadn't paid her income taxes for several years.
- A couple needs to pay off a mortgage and a line of credit, which will take years, because he decided he knew enough about investing their savings in the stock market simply from reading the newspaper and watching TV, then lost a bundle.
- He had been fired from multiple jobs because "he can't work with others" and now has trouble finding a job.
- It turned out she was not a "brilliant entrepreneur" who has simply had bad luck, but rather a serial business flop who is now about to go bankrupt for the second time.
- He bought an expensive time-share in South America on their joint credit card, but now they cannot afford the airfare needed to get to this country, so the investment was a waste of money.

- She doesn't have a credit card, not because she is against them (as she always says), but because her credit rating has been ruined and no institution will give her one.
- They can't buy a home because they don't qualify for a mortgage. He has a huge debt for unpaid taxes.

Many Canadians simply do not know how to manage money. Would you want to know that before or after you get married? I thought so. Bottom line: learn about your partner's financial situation, job history, bankruptcies, credit card history; do the equivalent of a credit check on them. One financial advisor refers to these kinds of financial problems as "FTDs." Instead of having sexually transmitted diseases, a couple experiences "financially transmitted diseases." Go into your marriage with eyes wide open; there should be no financial surprises.

~

Now, I realize that dealing with these issues may not be what many would view as an "enjoyable" or "easy" conversation to have with their partner. No one likes the idea of confronting their partner about the unpleasant details of their past, the personal and potentially upsetting health history of their family, or sensitive issues such as money management. But *do not* let it deter you from making a commitment to learn such details about your partner. I've seen too many relationships ruined because partners didn't make the effort to find out important details about each other's health, family history, and financial situation. When the gory details ultimately did emerge, they wished they had known sooner. You owe it to yourself and to your partner to make sure that you are both aware of any potentially serious issues that may arise. And this doesn't necessarily mean interrogating each other about the details. As a starting point, a little online research could be valuable—Google your future partner!

Certainly, you will learn some details by addressing them in an open conversation with your partner, but other details will come to light simply by being attentive. When you're at family functions, make an effort to talk to your partner's relatives and listen to stories they tell, and pay attention to the subjects that are no-no's. You may find out about a long-running family illness, or they may hint at a past problem that you can discuss later with your partner (for example, if relatives keep telling you that "You're the best thing that ever happened to him/her," find out why). Above all, what's important is that you are in a relationship in which you both appreciate the value of full disclosure and can have an open and honest conversation about such tough issues as a result of that disclosure. Ignore these important personal details at your peril!

So, let's assume that you have done your due diligence. You are now fully aware of all important issues and challenges in the relationship, and let's assume that you are now still committed to this relationship. What next? Are you ready to work at the relationship every day? In the next section, I provide some observations about ways to develop and maintain a good relationship

RELATIONSHIP BUILDING

I have seen my fair share of divorces and breakdowns in common-law relationships over the last three decades during which I've practised law. I have witnessed some very ugly separations and represented people in court battles over children, property, and money. I have seen couples spend hundreds of thousands of dollars on lawyers. I have seen weddings called off, children put in foster care, and their parents sent to jail. In some cases, I have helped grandparents fight their own children in order to get custody of their grandchildren, and I have seen it all up close, including blood, bruises, bankruptcy, and tears. And after it is all over, I have seen those same people pick themselves up, dust themselves off, and start over in a new relationship. Maybe I have only seen the relationships that have gone bad or people behaving at their absolute worst, but after witnessing the collapse of so many relationships, I have a better understanding of what can make or break a relationship.

One lesson that I have drawn from these observations is that couples rarely work at their relationships as hard as they do at their jobs, at their businesses, at their careers, and in some cases, even at their hobbies. They leave the success or failure of their relationships to chance. In this section I want to provide a little guidance on what

I think it takes to have a good relationship that is not only loving, but also durable. Let's start by taking a look at the 10 elements that make up the foundation of a good relationship:

1. honesty
2. patience
3. taking the long view
4. respect
5. balance
6. tolerance and forgiveness
7. room for growth
8. a sense of humour
9. loving gestures
10. effort

In my view, if any one of these key elements is missing then the love upon which the relationship is based is not mature and the relationship is therefore at risk. Are you or your partner dishonest, impatient, short-sighted, or disrespectful? Is one in the couple more powerful than the other? Are you forgiving? Is the relationship stagnant? Are you unable to laugh at yourselves? Is the relationship cold? Are you not prepared to work at it? If the answer is yes to any one of these, it can be fatal to the relationship.

What Makes for a Mature Relationship?

As a divorce lawyer for the last 30 years I have seen relationships both good and bad. I have seen the problems that eat away at a relationship, that undermine and corrode what might otherwise be a successful couple. In my view it depends in large part on whether the underlying love between the people is mature. In this section I invite you to consider some key components to a mature relationship.

1. Honesty

In my experience, dishonesty is the #1 cause of problems in relationships, and in many cases it begins long before the couple has made a decision to marry. I spoke earlier in this chapter about the need for due diligence. Hiding health problems, a criminal past, or financial problems as one goes into a relationship is dishonesty. Similarly, if those problems develop only after the relationship has begun but they are hidden from a spouse, then there is dishonesty within the relationship and it is at risk.

2. *Patience*

Patience means different things to different people. For some, it is as simple as waiting a few extra minutes for someone to come around to sharing their view. For others, patience can mean waiting an entire year for a situation within the relationship to evolve. In a good relationship, it means being patient for small things and for big things, and can mean giving your partner as much time as it takes him or her to do whatever it is that's important to them.

In one case that I saw, a man had to be very patient while his intelligent, beautiful, and well-educated wife decided what was important to her. Her life seemed to have been pre-determined for her; she was successful and happy. However, when she reached her fortieth birthday, she was suddenly unsure about what to do with her future. The things that she had worked on before did not seem important anymore and she needed time to decide what she would do next. After a couple of months, he became a little restless about her uncertainty. She had quit her job and they were missing her income. He was worried that she was slipping into a depression, but he waited and supported her as she worked out her priorities. And then suddenly, she had worked it out; it was time to become a teacher. She enrolled in teachers' college, attained her degree, and went on to become a happy teacher—and a happy partner. His patience was a virtue in that circumstance.

3. *Taking the Long View*

Therapists who assist couples spend a great deal of time trying to identify the indicators of a good relationship. They want to be able to tell people in therapy that this type of behaviour or that type of behaviour is good or bad. One of the good behaviours that they have identified is the ability to take the long view of the relationship. Where the individuals involved see their commitment as long term, they are better able to endure the little bumps that challenge them along the way. In fact, many successful couples acknowledge that the longer the relationship lasts and the more challenges they face successfully, the easier it is to roll over fresh obstacles.

Once I met a couple who described suffering a real blow early in their relationship. Just as they were preparing to embark on what they thought would be a happy, prosperous life together, the financial bottom fell out of the husband's successful business. It went bankrupt very suddenly, through no fault of his own. However, the couple worked through it, and all the stress that goes with financial problems. They rebuilt the business as partners and, as a result, the relationship became, in their mind, indestructible. They both felt that having been through the experience together, and taking the long view, they could now withstand any challenge.

4. Respect

Respect is so much bigger in a relationship than any dictionary definition could capture. What makes us hold our partner in a place of honour? Perhaps we see in them qualities that we admire, qualities that we wish we had. Respecting your partner may be something as basic as simply wanting to know what they think before you make a decision because you value the extra insight that they bring to a problem. Unfortunately, many couples appreciate the importance of respect only after it has disappeared.

I will never forget meeting a man who conveyed to me in an ashamed whisper that he and his wife were trying to work things out after his affair with a co-worker became public in a most humiliating way. The co-worker had launched into a drunken tirade against his wife at an office function. After the ugly incident, he was very remorseful and determined to set the matter right, but he knew that something was different with his wife. He sounded wounded as he described it to me: "She has no respect for me any more." A state of being held in honour was gone.

5. *Balance*

The old expression about everything in moderation certainly holds true for relationships. Whether it is the level of power between the two partners, their career objectives, or other activities, balance is always needed. I have seen couples separate because a husband's career became a single-minded obsession for him, or because a wife's devotion to a new religious faith became her sole purpose in life, and in one case, because a person's devotion to a new hobby—cycling—became the focal point of all his spare time. A balanced lifestyle is a solid foundation to a lasting relationship. Similarly, if one spouse begins to dominate the relationship or, on the other hand, one is not making an equal contribution, then other elements of the relationship may suffer as well. Will respect for a partner continue for very long if one dominates the other? Will there be room for growth? Why would spouses take the long view in a relationship if the relationship is not really about their life at all? Can people be honest in a relationship in which they have no power? Not for long.

6. *Tolerance and Forgiveness*

This aspect of relationship-building needs little explanation, but couples should understand that it is called for in the most subtle situations. The beauty of a relationship is the security and safety that I mentioned earlier. That security includes the freedom to make some mistakes as the relationship grows and as we grow as people, and know that one partner is still in your corner rooting for you, tolerating your shortcomings and sometimes, forgiving the booboos you make along the way.

7. *Room for Growth*

I don't think that our core values change very much over the course of our lives, but there are changes in us nonetheless. All of the challenges and experiences that one encounters over the course of a lifetime contribute to a person's growth as an individual. The hard part can be giving a partner the room to grow when it sometimes pushes you out of a comfortable routine. Imagine, for example, a powerful businessperson who had been in a relationship of 15 years suddenly developing a passionate interest in homelessness. An incident in his life had stirred up something dormant. He went from spending his evenings in a tux at business meetings and cocktail receptions to wearing a comfortable pair of corduroy pants and sweaters, while working in shelters for the homeless. Gradually, he began to apply all of his know-how and business savvy to the non-profit voluntary sector. His earnings took a hit but he had never been happier. His wife noticed a profound change, not only in his level of activity, but also in his level of happiness. He had not changed, but he had grown.

Life can settle into some comfortable grooves and we don't like to fiddle with a good thing. It is understandable that if one partner starts to rock the boat a little bit, then the other one may resist it. But if you are patient and flexible and allow that room to grow, it will pay dividends and you will both grow together.

8. *A Sense of Humour*

It helps to have a lot of laughter in one's life and it certainly helps relationships. The need for a sense of humour is most often called for in relation to one's self. In other words, we all need to be reminded not to take ourselves too seriously. A sense of humour can come to the rescue in the most difficult times.

9. *Loving Gestures*

In 1994, the results of a very interesting study of couples in marriage therapy were published. This study (called the Gottman study) was drawn from work done over a 20-year period with 2,000 couples and even involved the observation and measurement of their responses to each other while in therapy. Videotapes were examined to monitor facial expressions and language. The study was quite comprehensive and the results blew away many of the assumptions that marriage therapists and others have about which relationships will work and which ones won't. Gottman is so confident in his research that he claims he can predict with a 94-percent accuracy rate which relationships will end and which will not.

Gottman points out that we all tend to look at relationships in which there is a lot of arguing and shouting and assume "Well, that will never last—they argue too much." Likewise, it is not uncommon to hear friends and family say, "They're not compatible ... it's a different religion, a different ethnic background, a different class, different tastes. It can't last." These are not necessarily the indicators of a so-called good relationship. There is something else at work in the relationships; something inside the intimacy of the relationship itself.

One of the key findings of the Gottman study is the "Five-to-One Rule." Relationships are based on interactions between the couple, good and bad. Gottman found that he could quantify the ratio of positive to negative interactions needed to keep a relationship in good shape. He found that satisfied couples, no matter how their relationship stacked up against the ideal, were those who maintained a five-to-one ratio of positive to negative moments.

In the course of a day, there are opportunities for good and bad moments with your partner. Do you choose to tell your partner that they are attractive, or do you make a sarcastic remark about how they're not keeping in shape the way they used to? Do you encourage your partner to set aside time for themselves and their personal interests, or do you only remind them of their obligations and duties in the relationship? Do you make time for personal time away from the kids, or do you take turns handing off the responsibility until you each feel like rotating daycare shift workers. Do you smile at each other? Do you even look at each other? These are all the little positive and negative interactions of the day. Can you keep them in a ratio of five positives for every one negative? Can you afford not to? You can have a bad moment in a relationship, but you need to balance it with five good ones. It is a lot like keeping a healthy balance in the bank—some protection for a rainy day in the relationship.

10. Effort

Success in relationships, as in everything else, takes work. Couples cannot take their relationships for granted. The world throws a lot more at a couple these days than it did in the past. Be prepared to put in the effort, to be on guard, and to be ready to tackle the problems that will inevitably come.

Have Realistic Expectations

Let's take a look now at another aspect of having a good relationship—realistic expectations. During the course of any relationship, many things can and will happen. The following is a short list of things that I have actually seen happen to couples and that could just as easily happen to you:

- a serious illness—mental or physical
- injury in a car accident
- deafness or blindness
- termination of employment
- criminal activity and a resulting prison sentence
- addiction to drugs or alcohol
- money lost due to gambling
- a big lottery win
- transfer of employment to another country
- deportation
- an affair
- sexual abuse of a child
- an extended disappearance
- accidental death of a child due to drinking and driving

All of these things have happened to someone just like you. People in love say that they will be able to handle anything that comes their way. Could you handle some of the things on the above list? Some relationships rise to the challenge; many do not. The bottom line is this: having realistic expectations in a relationship does not mean that you are cynical or jaded about people and life. It means that you are simply aware that anything can happen—anything.

Having said that, let's look in particular at some of the more common challenges.

Money

Financial problems are quite common and often lead to stress in a relationship. Canadians have suffered from a record number of bankruptcies, job losses, and debt levels and the recent economic troubles have really taken a toll on Canadian families. No one likes to tell their partner or their children that they can't have a computer, that their vacation is cancelled, that the car cannot be repaired, or that the house has to be sold. Poor finances make people feel trapped and helpless.

On the other side of the coin, we have couples who have problems because they have too much money—that's right, too much. I saw a couple with children blow apart because they could not handle a lot of money that came into their hands very suddenly. Before long, the money was gone—and so was the marriage. Couples need to have realistic expectations and all couples, especially younger ones, should get some basic financial planning advice. Speak to your bank representative, follow the advice of trusted friends, and shop around for someone who is qualified, experienced, and honest to advise you on financial matters. There are many very good financial planners out there (check out, for example, www.fpsc.ca). Something as simple as a good working financial budget can make a big difference in eliminating stress in a relationship.

What follows is a list of 10 tips that are designed to help make it easier to find a financial planner, courtesy of the Financial Planner Standards Council (www.fpsccanada.org):

- Know what you want. Determine your general financial goals and specific needs, such as insurance, estate planning, and investment planning.
- Be prepared. Do a little research on financial planning strategies and terminology.
- Get advisor referrals from colleagues and friends.
- Look for competence. There are many degrees and designations. The Financial Planner Standards Council recommends a planner with a CFP designation (Certified Financial Planner).
- Interview more than one planner. Ask about their education, experience and specialties, the size and duration of their practice, client communications, and whether assistants handle client matter.
- Check their background. Call their professional associations to check on their complaint record.

- Ask for references from other professionals, such as accountants, insurance agents, or legal advisors who work with the planner.
- Ask for a registration or disclosure document detailing the method of compensation, conflicts of interest, business affiliations, and personal qualifications.
- Request a written advisory contract or engagement letter.
- Reassess the relationship regularly.

Children

Ideally, a couple should decide before they commit to their relationship about the question of raising a family together. The realistic expectation here is simply this: if you cannot agree in advance about whether you both want to have children, under no circumstances should you get married, and it should put a real question mark over whether you want to live in a common-law relationship until the issue is sorted out—honestly.

Relatives

You will recall from the above list of characteristics that contribute to a good relationship the need for patience and tolerance. This may have no greater application than when one is dealing with in-laws. The need to have some realistic expectations can arise in a couple of different situations. You may have heard the expression "the sandwich generation"—these are Canadians in their thirties, forties, fifties, and sixties who are sandwiched in between caring for their own children and their aging parents, and in some cases, grandparents. This group will grow larger and larger over the next few decades, and it will mean an extra strain on many relationships. Imagine trying to squeeze into an already crowded schedule the need to pop into a nursing home to care for your mother or father. In many cases, they may be living right in your home, creating an additional expense for nursing care. Now, imagine that it is not you but your spouse who must add the extra care onto the daily routine. Remember the comfortable routine and the room for growth we talked about earlier? Both can evaporate in this kind of heat.

Studies of this growing social issue have shown that parental care generally falls to the women in the family. We already know that women are still doing the majority of the housework and childcare, and when eldercare is added to the situation, it will feel less like a sandwich and more like a vise. Take a look at your own situation and that of your spouse. How would you handle that kind of responsibility? Talk about it.

A second in-law issue is the one on which many comedians have made a living: the dreaded in-laws who meddle and try to run their children's lives after they start their relationships. Unfortunately, the jokes have a basis in reality, and I have seen some terrible interference in relationships by parents. Rarely do all four parents get into it; more often than not, the strong personalities in the parents' marriages are the ones who try to become overly involved in their children's relationships.

As you head into a relationship you have to have realistic expectations about family members who will intervene in your life together. Ideally, you have had a chance to meet the families involved and size them up. A relative who meddles and tries to control their child before the marriage even begins will not suddenly stop doing so after you are married. For example, if a young man has lived in his parents' basement for 10 years, saving his money up for a nice car, while his mother does the cooking and cleaning for him, don't expect things to be much different once a marriage begins. Have realistic expectations about your relationship—not just with your partner, but with your partner's family.

Careers

The need for realistic expectations in our careers doesn't need much explanation to most Canadians. We have all been through the recent economic difficulties and understand the way in which global markets can turn our economy upside-down overnight. We hear constant warnings about flu pandemics, terrorism, and other threats around the globe. The situation can be rosy one day and suddenly go quite sour. We need to have realistic expectations about the security of our own financial position.

A neighbour of mine sold his house on the condition that the purchasers could arrange financing within 72 hours. That is a pretty common condition in a house transaction; however, when the intended purchaser went to her employer to get a letter for the bank confirming her earnings, she got a pink slip instead. She lost her dream home and her job in the same day. Be realistic about what can happen to your career and how it can affect your plans.

Illness

I mentioned this aspect of relationships earlier in the context of due diligence. It can be a shocker when a relationship has to face illness or injury (and let's not forget that it's a dangerous world out there—car accidents, workplace accidents, crime, and other dangers are all around us). It would be a miracle if we got through life without something happening. When we consider the thousands of illnesses from which Canadians suffer, physically and mentally, it can be a little overwhelming.

Having realistic expectations in a relationship means understanding that these things could happen to you or your spouse. Could you cope? Could your partner? There are couples who simply cannot deal with these kinds of challenges. I once met with a client whose wife had left him the day after he was diagnosed with cancer. For whatever reason, she could not handle the prospect of seeing him through that ordeal. And that case is not an isolated one. Lawyers see many cases in which illness or injury end a relationship. It is sad, but true. The bottom line is to be realistic about what life can and will throw at you as an individual and as a couple.

Develop Good Problem-Solving Skills

Good problem-solving skills are about having the ability to handle reality when it hits day after day. Marriage therapists and lawyers will tell you that the best indicator of whether a relationship will be successful is not the challenges of money, sex, or any of the usual problems we often associate with relationships. It is the willingness and ability of both partners to work on problems and to solve them. Then it won't matter what is thrown your way, because if you work on solving the problem together, your relationship has a good chance of being successful. Don't wish that you won't have problems, because that is unrealistic. Wish instead that you will have the ability to work on them together when they arrive—and trust me, they will.

Ten Elements of Good Problem Solving

There is an approach to problem solving that can be of great assistance to a couple in their marriage. It is simple and it consists of identifying the real problem and its origins, proposing alternative solutions, evaluating those alternatives, picking the one that meets both spouses' needs, and then implementing it. Let's look at it in more detail through the following 10 elements.

1. What is the problem?

As a couple, you should be prepared to ask really simple questions about the challenges or problems that you think you face. Do you both come up with the same answer? Let me give you an example. If a couple is facing serious financial problems and they ask themselves what the problem really is, they may not get the same answer. The husband might say that the problem is "We don't earn enough money and I need a better paying job." The wife, on the other hand, might say, "We spend too much on things that we don't need, things that are not important or that we cannot afford. Let's keep our jobs and spend less." They don't see the same problem and they cannot begin to solve it until they agree on what the problem truly is.

2. How did this problem arise?

What is its source? It can be very helpful to trace the origin of a problem. Has this come up before? Why is it happening again? Are we repeating mistakes that have been made before? For example, if overspending led to an enormous debt, and the debt was then consolidated into a new mortgage on the home in the past, but now another period of overspending has allowed another debt to balloon, did the consolidation really solve the underlying problem? If the couple can pin down the source of the problem, they may prevent the problem from happening again.

3. What are the facts of which we are absolutely certain?

A couple cannot possibly hope to solve a problem if they do not have all of the facts surrounding the issue. This means that, in analyzing the problem, the couple must ask, "Do we have enough information?" Remember the advice about honesty in the relationship. It applies here as well. All of the facts need to be on the table for a proper solution to be developed.

4. Once all of the facts have been gathered, does the problem look the same?

Don't be surprised if it looks a lot different after a true picture has been assembled. This means that once you have all of the facts in hand, go back to the question that we started with: "What is the problem?"

5. What are the timelines we face in solving this problem?

Are they rigid or flexible? The way that you choose to solve the problem and the alternatives that you may consider will be influenced by the time limits imposed by others. If a creditor is forcing your hand, then making a career change to earn more money may not be realistic. If one of you has been offered a job in another country and must give an answer by a certain date, then your choices are limited. Be aware of time restrictions on your decision making.

6. What are the alternative ways in which we can solve this problem?

Never assume that there is only one solution because, more often than not, there are several ways to solve the problem. A couple of the solutions may not seem suitable, but they are at least possibilities. Be open-minded, brainstorm about possibilities, think out loud, and imagine the best solution if it were entirely up to you. Don't be afraid to involve other professionals, such as financial planners, lawyers, or your accountant in developing a solution.

7. What are the pros and cons of each alternative?

This can be quite a useful exercise as you both work at listing the advantages and disadvantages of each potential solution. Sometimes, you will be surprised at how easily the best alternative emerges.

8. Which alternative makes the most sense?

Depending on the kind of problem you face, the option that looks the best to you might not be the same for your partner. It will be necessary to consider what is best for the relationship, rather than what is best for you as individuals.

9. What does my partner think?

Hopefully you will both have the same information in front of you, have identified the same problem, have considered the same options, and considered the same pros and cons for each option. This is the time to make sure that each partner is given an opportunity to say what he or she thinks about a possible solution. Don't jump to conclusions and start figuring out how to implement the solution unless you are certain that both of you are committed to implementing it.

10. Are we committed to implementing the solution?

Assuming that you are both on the same wavelength about the best alternative to solve the problem, you must both commit yourselves to working on implementation. Finding the correct approach is only half the answer. It must still be implemented and it must be implemented together. Leaving the problem solving to just one partner will create an imbalance in the relationship and may very well lead to a repetition of the mistake that got you into the problem in the first place.

~

In this chapter we looked at why a lot of relationships go sour. Good relationships are built from the bottom up based on mature love, realistic expectations, and good problem-solving skills. Couples can learn to have realistic expectations and they can learn to be good problem solvers, but when it comes to having the mature love required as a foundation, there are some limitations on how much can be learned. A person is either committed to those elements of a mature love—or not. I hope that some of the questions posed in this chapter will help you as a couple in evaluating each other and in evaluating the challenges that you face over the years together.

3

YOUR RIGHTS AND RESPONSIBILITIES TO EACH OTHER IF YOU ARE MARRIED BUT DO NOT HAVE A MARRIAGE CONTRACT

In this chapter, I would like you to become aware of what you are getting into simply by making the decision to marry. We will not be looking, at this stage, at what happens if there is a separation and divorce or a death of one of the spouses. Instead, what I would like to focus on are the spouses' rights and responsibilities to each other and to children while the marriage is intact. In other words, no matter how successful your marriage is, there are some things to think about and complications that may arise while you are married.

The introductory words to Ontario's *Family Law Act* are interesting. The preamble to the legislation states as follows:

> Whereas it is desirable to encourage and strengthen the role of the family; and whereas for that purpose it is necessary to recognize the equal position of spouses as individuals within marriage and to recognize marriage as a form of partnership; and whereas in

> support of such recognition it is necessary to provide in law for the orderly and equitable settlement of the affairs of the spouses upon the breakdown of the partnership and to provide for other mutual obligations in family relationships including the equitable sharing by parents of responsibility for their children.

Marriage is, of course, the ultimate romantic act, but it also sounds a lot like a business arrangement: two people are entering a partnership. According to the preamble, they are supposed to occupy equal positions in that partnership; they have mutual obligations to each other and to children. In this chapter we will look at how this partnership concerns the family's property, the treatment of children, financial obligations, and even planning for the future.

THE SIGNIFICANCE OF THE DATE OF THE MARRIAGE

The wedding day is often referred to as "the Big Day." I suppose for some the "big" concerns the cost of the wedding, but from a legal perspective, it is a big day because that is when the partnership begins. So from that day, some important questions arise:

- How will this partnership operate?
- Who will take responsibility for the finances of the family?
- What are the couple's attitudes about children?
- What are the couple's attitudes about acquiring and managing property?

More often than not, it is problems about finances that undermine marriages, and yet, very little thought or planning is put into how the family partnership will be managed.

As we saw in the previous chapter, couples need to do due diligence on each other prior to marriage. If you have entered this partnership with someone who has a track record of financial mismanagement, I assure you that a marriage certificate will not suddenly turn him or her into a model financial citizen. The causes of financial mismanagement often run deep and cannot be changed overnight. It will be difficult to have a happy and successful marriage if you run into problems like these:

- Dave and Mary have been married for two years and Mary is concerned that Dave has not filed an income-tax return for as long as she can remember. She has been saving to contribute to a down payment on a home. When she spoke to a bank manager about financing for a home, he mentioned the need for proof that income taxes had been paid. Whenever she raises the subject of income taxes with Dave, he is evasive.
- Ralph and Maria have been married for four years and are thinking about starting a family. They have talked about planning an extended vacation before settling in to raise their family. Maria cashed in her RRSPs to pay for the vacation without speaking to Ralph.
- Craig and Jean have been married for 18 months. They want to buy a home but Jean is reluctant to commit until she has paid off her student loans. Her parents have loaned them the money for a down payment, but Jean is thinking of using that money to pay off the student loans first.

You can see from the above examples that tension around finances can easily cause trouble. At this stage you need to be aware that things change as of the date of marriage.

Each spouse needs to be aware of what the other is bringing into the partnership, whether it be assets or liabilities. Assets can range from furniture and vehicles to a home that was owned before the marriage. Liabilities can include student loans, credit card debt, and loans from family members. It can be particularly valuable, as we will see, for the couple to have a good idea about the financial starting point for their marriage, a taking stock as of the big day. This will allow the couple to make a financial game plan to strengthen the marriage. It is possible for a marriage contract to assist in that strengthening process.

Let's turn now to a consideration of something even more important than the marriage's finances: children.

WHAT ABOUT HAVING CHILDREN?

No one needs a marriage licence to have children, but it is certainly one of the most significant decisions that a couple can make. As discussed in the previous chapter, the desire for children and a commitment to have them is something that should be discussed well in advance of the wedding. In my own practice, I recently had the unpleasant task of helping a young couple separate and dissolve their marriage because the husband blurted out over dinner one night that he did not support the idea of having children—never had and never would. This comment was made despite the fact that they had dated for several years, lived together common law, and carefully planned a large, expensive wedding. From the wife's perspective: Why be married if there would never be children? She should have discovered her husband's views on children much earlier.

Canadians who marry need to think about children in two possible contexts. First, having their own biological children, but also blending children from a previous relationship. Remarriage is creating thousands of blended families and this blending is creating all kinds of interesting questions and challenges for families. Step-parenting can be complicated. First and foremost, there will probably be another biological parent involved in the lives of the children. Perhaps that parent has joint custody or access to the children on a regular basis and the time the children spend with the newly married family will be interrupted regularly. If there are two sets of children being blended into a new marriage, then coordination of three or more households may be required. Discipline can also be an issue, especially when there are two or more different styles of parenting and children see an inconsistent approach depending on which household they are in. One parent is sometimes viewed as being too harsh or as spoiling the children. It is very delicate and it calls for patience and diplomacy with the children, with the biological parent, and with your new spouse.

Parents have a financial obligation to provide the necessities of life to each other and to their children while married. This means that food, shelter, medical, and clothing needs must be met. Provincial law states that while married, a spouse has authority to render himself or herself and his or her spouse jointly and severally liable to a third party for the necessities of life unless the spouse has notified the third party that he or she has withdrawn the authority. You have perhaps seen those curious little ads in the classified section of the newspaper that state "Bill Brown will not be responsible for the debts of Betty Brown." These are ads which are supposed to be evidence to the world that Bill Brown will not be responsible for any bills or debts incurred by his wife Betty. It is his notice to third parties that he has withdrawn the authority to incur expenses on behalf of the family. However, as long as the family is intact, either spouse can incur debt to make sure that the family has food, shelter, and clothing, and that medical needs are being met.

If a couple marries and blends children into a new family, a question arises: What is the non-biological parent's obligation for his or her spouse's children while the family is intact? Married couples often adopt their partner's children from a previous relationship. This has the effect of terminating the other biological parent's obligations with respect to the child. In many families, however, the children are simply blended together and no adoption takes place. The biological parent's obligations, with respect to that child, continue.

Step-parents who have not adopted their partner's children technically have no rights with respect to those children, but they may have responsibilities: for the most part, the step-parent cannot be forced to pay for the child's schooling or medical needs; he or she cannot go to the children's school and remove the child from school property; and he or she cannot remove the child from Canada without the permission of the child's biological parents. If the spouse, however, has sole custody of their children, as they enter the blended relationship, then that parent can delegate responsibility to the step-parent (e.g., provide a letter authorizing the parent to remove the child from school property or even from the country), but this is an authority given by the parent. There are no direct rights vis-à-vis the child for the step-parent.

This can sometimes be an issue in terms of discipline. Does a step-parent have any more authority over their partner's children other than that to which the biological parent agrees or to which the child consents? Morally there may be authority, perhaps. Legally, no. The relationship between step-parents and stepchildren can be tricky, but, as we will see, it is also something that can benefit from clarification in a marriage contract.

Financially, caring for children varies from family to family and depends largely on the parents' respective abilities to contribute financially. If incomes are equal, life may be a little less complicated.

However, when the couple involves a blended family and the spouse with children is receiving child support from the child's biological parent, finances can become more complicated. The parent paying child support does so based on his or her gross annual income. The income of the parent receiving child support is not relevant to the base monthly amount that is paid for child support, nor is the income of the new legal spouse relevant to the calculation of child support. We will examine this calculation in more detail in an upcoming chapter, but for now consider the following example:

- Tom and Cindy married, Tom for the first time and Cindy for the second. Cindy has three children from her first marriage with Gary. Gary has regular access to the children and pays child support to Cindy based on his gross annual income of $144,800. His monthly tax-free payment to Cindy for child support is $2,504 for the three children. This is calculated in order to cover the children's food, shelter, clothing and other basic needs. Cindy on the other hand earns about $130,000 a year, and she and Gary split equally all of the other special expenses related to the children's music lessons, dance lessons, and swimming. This has resulted in Gary providing an additional $3,000 per year for the children's extra-curricular activities. Gary's total payments to Cindy per year for child support are therefore 12 payments of $2,504 plus $3,000 for a grand total of $33,048 per year. This money is tax free in Cindy's hands and not tax deductible to Gary.
- How do Tom and Cindy manage Gary's financial contribution to their household? Gary will have no input into how Cindy spends the child support. Courts have been reluctant to allow parents who pay child support to dictate how it is to be spent. How does Cindy manage the child support in a way that maximizes the intended benefits to her children? Can tension between Tom and Gary be avoided as Gary feels he subsidizes the new marriage? For some families it may mean something as simple as a deposit of the entire child support directly into a joint account with no discussion about how it is spent. Other families may parse out the child support into RESP accounts, children's savings, clothing, allowances, budgets for school, and so on. Every family has different ways of approaching this.

- If both spouses are receiving child support from previous relationships, allocation can become even more complicated especially when incomes of the payor spouses are very different and therefore the amounts of child support being paid for the respective children varies widely. Imagine, for example, in the Tom and Cindy scenario, if Tom had three children from his previous relationship and was receiving child support from his previous spouse. If his previous spouse earned $40,400 per year, her contribution for the three children she had with Tom would be $782 per month. In other words, Tom is contributing to the new household budget, support from his partner of less than $800 a month for his three children, while Cindy's former partner, Gary, is contributing over $3,000 a month for her children. It can be tricky ensuring that everyone is treated fairly.

Another common scenario is the situation faced by a couple when one spouse is a recipient of child support and one spouse is a payor of child support. Consider the following example:

> Phil is divorced from Patty and pays her $900 per month for child support for their two children. Phil has now married Amanda. She receives $900 per month for child support from her former common-law partner, Allan, for their one child. Money flows into the household budget and money flows out. Is Allan simply paying Phil's child support obligation to Patty? No, of course not, but it may feel like that. You can see that child support in fully functioning blended families can be a source of friction.

As we will see in Chapter 6, many of these issues can be addressed in a marriage contract, but they highlight some of the financial issues faced by couples with blended families. (Of course, it becomes even more complicated if one spouse is also receiving spousal support).

WHAT ABOUT BUYING PROPERTY?

We do not think of it day to day, but as we acquire property—cars, furniture, electronic entertainment systems, sports equipment, pots and pans, and even real estate—there is technical legal ownership of these assets. In other words, a person who acquires property is the legal owner of the item and is entitled to have the law support their ownership rights. This may mean, for example, forcing the item of property to be returned to them if it has been taken. It could mean pledging the asset as security for a loan. This could range from something as simple as taking your guitar to a pawn shop to a million-dollar mortgage on a recreational property or a business. Ownership also means the right to sell objects outright. In this section, I hope to clarify the impact of marriage on a spouse's ability to deal with assets that they own. Let's consider some examples.

- Andy and Marilyn have been married for several years. Andy has a successful printing business. He is thinking of expanding and has approached the bank for a line of credit. According to principles of family law, Andy and Marilyn are in a "partnership" in their marriage. Does this mean that Marilyn must consent to Andy obtaining financing for his business expansion?
- Certainly Marilyn will be interested in the success of Andy's business decision. If it turns out to be a poor time to expand and Andy cannot repay the loan, then the entire financial security of the family could be undermined, and yet Marilyn has no ability to have input on this decision. Any asset that is in the name of Andy alone is an asset that he is free to deal with in any way that he chooses, regardless of the impact that it may have on him or the family. If Andy owns a car, he may sell it; if he has RRSPS and he wishes to cash them in to buy a motorcycle, he may do so. Just because a couple marries, does not mean that asserts that are in their name cannot be dealt with as they choose.
- Bob and Susan have been married for five years. They acquired a beautiful home in an up-and-coming part of Toronto. Given the value of their home, there may be as much as $500,000 equity available for investment. The property is registered in the name of Bob alone. On the weekend Bob saw a beautiful recreational property that can be acquired for $200,000. He approaches the bank manager and asks for a loan of $200,000 to be secured against the home that is registered in his name alone. The bank manager asks if the home, although registered in Bob's name alone, is a matrimonial home, in other words, the home in which Bob resides with a legally married spouse.

- When Bob explains that yes, indeed, he does live there with his wife Susan, the bank informs him that Susan will need to consent to an increase in any financing registered against the home. This is because a matrimonial home is an exception to the rule about legally married spouses being able to deal with assets that are registered in their name alone. The matrimonial home is considered the most important financial asset acquired by a family and it is therefore given special protection.

For the most part, couples acquire property without paying attention to title. Sometimes one person buys the flat-screen TV and someone else buys the new bicycles or the family car. In some cases the ownership is joint, and both names appear on the ownership; in some cases there is no formal ownership or proof beyond perhaps a credit-card slip. All of these assets are held and dealt with by the couple as the marriage evolves. In some cases, assets may be dealt with freely, but in the case of a matrimonial home, special protection is afforded.

WHAT ABOUT INCOME AND EXPENSES?

As mentioned earlier, this is an area that justifies a red alert as management of income and payment of expenses is a source of friction in marriages. Couples have a variety of ways of managing their income and expenses:

- In some cases a joint bank account is used into which all income is deposited.
- In other relationships, separate bank accounts are maintained.
- In some relationships one person may have a particular aptitude for managing the finances and the other has no interest whatsoever.
- In some cases, responsibility is shared and, more often than not, no one is really taking care of the money and problems arise.

Whether it is done so consciously or not, an understanding is usually reached by the couple about how much it costs to run their household and the respective contributions are made to cover those costs. As long as the couple is in agreement, the system works. As long as each person in the couple is employed, the system works. Unfortunately that agreement is often undermined by mismanagement or changes in a spouse's ability to contribute. Again this is where a marriage contract can work wonders for managing any agreement needed with respect to income and allocation of expenses.

WHAT ABOUT MEDICAL/DENTAL HEALTH BENEFITS?

Once married, all public and private health care plans allow the designation of a legally married spouse for the purposes of accessing the plan. Entitlement to benefits is immediate and there is no qualifying period.

WHAT ABOUT INCOME TAX RETURNS?

Once married, couples are able to use a variety of income-tax provisions available to spouses. I suggest that you go to the Canada Revenue Agency website http://www.cra-arc.gc.ca for exact up-to-date information relevant to spouses.

WHAT ABOUT WILLS AND POWERS OF ATTORNEY?

All couples require wills. If the will is not in place at the time of a person's death, that person is considered to have died intestate and it becomes necessary to use what is known as the "succession law" of the province in which that person resides in order to determine how their property will be allocated among surviving family.

If a person is legally married, his or her surviving legal spouse has an automatic entitlement under provincial law through what is known as a "preferential share" in the estate. After a surviving legal spouse receives his or her preferential share, the balance is then divided again between the spouse and any children. A situation of intestacy creates tension and expense for a surviving family. It is even worse for common-law spouses who do not always automatically have an entitlement to share in the estate of a deceased spouse. This has meant that, in some cases when common-law partners died without a will in place, the surviving common-law spouse was left to fight with the deceased's children from a previous relationship or with a previous legally married spouse of the deceased, siblings of the deceased, and even the deceased's parents.

All couples, whether common law or legally married, would be well advised to have wills in place to deal with the potential financial dependency of their survivors, guardianship of their children, and distribution of their property. If a spouse dies, his or her property will need to be distributed. His or her debts will need to be paid, and if possible, directions will need to be given for the funeral, donation of organs, and other related issues. It should be clear from the foregoing sections that directions as to who gets what is never more important than at the time of a person's death.

We will be looking at the consequences of death for legally married couples in Chapter 5, but at this stage the key thing to remember is that, as a couple, whether at the beginning of your marriage or if your marriage is well underway, you must have wills and powers of attorney in place to manage this critical time.

The same is true with respect to Powers of Attorney for Personal Care and Property. (These documents are known by different names in various provinces but have the same legal effect.) For example, in British Columbia they are referred to as "mandates." These documents are legal authority for a person to make decisions on behalf of an individual if they are not in a position to make the decision themselves.

So, what have we learned from the foregoing sections about rights and responsibilities to each other while married?

- The date of your marriage is the beginning of a partnership.
- It is important that each spouse is aware of what the other partner is bringing to the relationship.
- The assets and liabilities of each spouse as of the day that you marry should be declared in full.
- The debt each spouse is bringing into the relationship should be declared.
- The spouses-to-be should discuss what impact those assets and liabilities will have on the marriage.

- Each spouse is free to acquire and deal with property freely during the course of the marriage. The exception to this rule is a matrimonial home, whether it is registered in the name of both spouses or only one. A matrimonial home may not be transferred or encumbered without the permission of both spouses.
- Having children is always a joyous event for a marriage. Each parent has a financial obligation to provide the necessities of life to their children and each other, to the best of their ability.
- Blended families create some challenges for their children particularly as support for children or for spouses flows in and out. Tensions can be created with the biological parent of a child in a blended family, and resentments can arise around the use of child support and spousal support payments. These tensions should be addressed head on and not allowed to undermine the marriage.
- Couples should be alive to the need for careful management of their incomes and allocation of those incomes to expenses. This is a number-one source of friction and problems in relationships. Budgeting and working with a financial advisor is absolutely critical to the financial well-being of the family.
- Legally married couples need to apply their minds not only to income tax benefits and planning but also to estate planning. This means ensuring that wills and powers of attorney are in place.

Let's turn now to a further reality check on marriage and the following questions:

- What happens when the relationship ends?
- What if you separate?
- What if you cannot agree on your rights and obligations to each other at the time of separation?
- What will the law do or not do for you?

By understanding the impact of the law on separation, divorce, and even on the death of a spouse, you as a couple will be better positioned to understand what steps you can take to strengthen the relationship through the use of a marriage contract.

4

THE LEGAL CONSEQUENCES OF MARRIAGE: RIGHTS AND RESPONSIBILITIES IF YOU SEPARATE

In Canada we have 10 Provinces, the Northwest Territories, Yukon, Nunavut, and a slightly different method of handling the treatment of legally married couples when they separate in each jurisdiction. Before you get too discouraged at the thought of figuring out how a particular Province's or Territory's law could apply to you, there are definitely a number of common approaches to the issues faced by couples at the time of separation or death of a spouse. Custody, access to children, child support and even spousal support all enjoy some uniformity. Property division, on the other hand, is different from province to province. In this chapter we will examine each of the key areas, look at examples of actual cases, and examine the common approaches. The goal is to inform you about what happens to legally married spouses who separate and do not have marriage contracts in place. Let's begin with an important question.

WHEN ARE YOU SEPARATED?

You will recall from the discussion at the opening of Chapter 3 in the section The Significance of the Date of Marriage, that the date of the start of your partnership is important. Similarly, the date upon which you separate is also important, particularly with respect to division of property. It can, however, be a difficult date for some couples to pin down. The actual moment of a relationship ending can seem like a moving target. To end a relationship there must be evidence of a desire and action by at least one of the parties to terminate it. If both people agree that, for example, the big argument they had on New Year's Eve and the fact that one person has moved out is evidence that the relationship was over on January 1, then the actual point of separation will not be difficult to pin down. But what if both of them have not applied their minds to the question? What if one person considers the relationship over? What if the other person thinks that, while the relationship is in trouble, counselling may save it? Are they separated?

Consider the following first interview with a spouse who thinks the marriage has been over for several months.

"When did you separate?"

"Last summer the relationship ended completely."

"What happened last summer?"

"We had an argument about whether to have children. When we couldn't agree we stopped having sex, so it was over."

"So the last time the two of you were intimate was last summer?"

"Yes, except for her birthday at a friend's cottage and once at Christmas and New Year's Eve but it really ended last summer when we were both feeling very unhappy."

"When did you tell your family that you were separating?"

"Uh, we didn't."

"When did you tell your friends?"

"Uh, we didn't."

"Did you tell any of your co-workers?"

"No."

"Is she still on your medical/dental plan?"

"Yes."

"If I asked your neighbours, what would they say?"

"Uh, nothing. They don't know anything about the separation."

"Are you eating meals together, doing your laundry together, and so on?"

"Yes, but…."

"Does she know you are here?"

"No way."

"If she was sitting here and I asked her what she thinks, what would she say?"

"She would want to work on the marriage by going to counselling."

Does that sound like a real-life situation? Yes. Do they sound like they are separated? No. Separation does not mean that both people agree that they are separated. It takes two to begin a relationship, but only one to end it. However, both people must be aware that one of them is actually calling it quits. Consider the following model conversation.

"Sarah, we need to talk about where we are going with this relationship."

"We are not splitting up Allan."

"I have spoken with a lawyer and…."

"You what?!"

"I have spoken with a lawyer and our relationship is over. I want to have an amicable discussion about what we do next to move on with our lives and still be friends."

"No way, I don't agree."

"I'm sorry."

This is a clear separation conversation, both are aware and one has acted in a decisive way. If that conversation was confirmed in writing, for example, by email, it would be conclusive proof that the relationship had come to an end.

Now we all know that conversations aren't always that articulate or clear. More often than not the couples allow an unhappy relationship to drift along. They are unhappy, they snipe at each other, intimacy dies; they keep busy and away from each other. They are afraid to confront what needs to be done; and then one person in the relationship does something, consciously or unconsciously, to deal a fatal blow to the relationship—an affair, an abusive argument, violence, something hurtful or embarrassing. And then nothing can be said or done to deny that it's over. It is a sad way to end a relationship, and yet, this is how many couples do it.

This is a good opportunity to put to rest a confusing bit of language that lawyers hear from clients: "We're not legally separated." As lawyers, we always scratch our heads and wonder what clients mean by that expression "legally separated." It implies that people could be "illegally" separated. There is no such terminology. You are either separated or not. I think that what clients probably mean is that the relationship is over, but they have not sorted out their legal issues by way of an agreement or a court order.

It is possible to be separated, even though you continue under the same roof. Consider the example of the model conversation set out above and imagine at the end of it the husband adds, "We cannot afford to separate and live in two apartments right now. Our lease is up in six months, so I think we should give our notice and start looking for new places of our own." If they then continue at the same address until the lease expires they will still be considered to be separated and the relationship over. There are many cases in which Canadian courts have found a couple to have been separated, even though they continued under the same roof.

We will see in a few minutes why pinpointing this date of separation is very important to the determination of a division of property, the calculation of spousal support, and other issues that need to be addressed when couples split up. The importance of the date is the same regardless of where you live—and separate—in Canada.

WHAT HAPPENS IF WE HAVE CHILDREN AND SEPARATE?

Custody and Access

Custody and access questions at the time of separation are among the most emotional. If the way in which the relationship ends is painful or unpleasant, it often contaminates the way in which a couple decides to make post-separation decisions about their children.

Consider Jake, age 40, and Renée, age 35. They were married seven years and had two children who are now six and four. The last year was rough because Renée had been ill. She had just started back to work, when she learned that Jake had been having an affair with a sales rep from a company with which he does business. Renée had been to business dinners with Jake and this young woman, Allison, age 30. Now she feels angry and humiliated. Jake has moved out to live with Allison and her two children. He wants to take his new girlfriend and all of the children on a vacation. As you can well imagine, it may be difficult for Renée and Jake to come to an agreement about custody and access with that kind of context to their relationship breakdown.

If they cannot agree, the court will be forced to step in and make custody and access orders. "Custody" means being given complete care and control of the children and the equivalent of visiting time to the other parent, called "access." What will the court consider in the circumstances of separation (regardless whether the couple is legally married or common law) in trying to decide what would be appropriate for the children after separation? The court focuses on one overarching goal—protecting the best interests of the children. What kinds of factors does a court consider when looking at a child's best interests? Consider the following:

- the relationship between the child and any person claiming custody or access to the child
- the relationship of the child to other members of that family (for example, siblings)
- the child's relationship to other people involved in that child's care and upbringing (for example, day-care workers and grandparents, as well as aunts and uncles)

- the child's views and preferences, provided those views and preferences can be reasonably ascertained (this usually means children who are over the age of 10)
- the length of time the child has lived in a stable home environment
- the ability and willingness of each person seeking custody or access to provide the child with guidance, education and the necessaries of life, or to meet any special needs that the child may have
- proposed plans for the child's care and upbringing
- the ability of a person to act as a parent to this child
- the relationship by blood or through an adoption order between the child and other people involved in the Court Application
- past conduct of a person, if the court is satisfied that the conduct is relevant to that person's ability to act as a parent
- whether the people applying for custody or access have at any time committed violence or abuse against a spouse, a parent, a member of the person's household, or the child himself or herself

Unfortunately, parents often do not realize until too late in the proceedings that a court is not particularly interested in behaviour that does not affect the ability to parent. So, for example, Jake's affair with Allison has absolutely nothing to do with his ability to parent the two children involved. If the situation involves a blended family, the court will be concerned with maintaining a relationship between the biological child and parent. However, there is no automatic entitlement to custody and the courts have been prepared to award custody of a child to a non-biological step-parent, if the biological parent is unable to look after the child's best interests. At the very least, a step-parent does have an opportunity to ask for access to the children post-separation.

At the end of these enquiries, which may be assisted by third-party investigators (such as social workers, private assessors, psychiatrists, psychologists, lawyers for the children, and even Children's Aid Societies), a determination is made that is presumably in the best interests of the children. These third party investigations (which may cost thousands of dollars) will examine everything from relationships with grandparents, the child's education and school experience, the child's circle of friends, sports and hobbies, and other extracurricular activities and then compare how each parent participates in those aspects of the child's life. A report is prepared with recommendations that the court should try to "preserve the child's universe" as much as possible.

The court has some limited options available to it when dealing with custody of children. In some cases parents agree that one parent should have custody and the other should have access. But more modern families, where both parents have been involved with the children's upbringing, often use concepts such as joint custody, shared parenting, or parallel parenting to manage the care of the children after separation.

In the case of joint custody, the parents share time with the children and responsibilities for their upbringing. The same is true with shared parenting, where the parents co-operate, in some cases simply replicating what they did while together but from separate houses. The mother will look after getting the children to medical and dental appointments, and the father will look after getting them to their recreational activities and music lessons. Parallel parenting has been a relatively recent development. It involves parents who have difficulty communicating with each other, but are prepared to try to parent their children in the absence of any direct parental co-operation. This means that in the mother's home a set of rules is developed, the children abide by those rules, and the mother accepts certain responsibilities while the children are with her. The children then move to the father's home, where the father has a set of rules (which we hope are at least similar to the mother's). The father then takes responsibility for the children while they are with him. While this form of parallel parenting continues, the parents do not communicate with each other. Each of the above options is available to common-law parents.

Other issues that need to be sorted out after separation include developing a schedule of time for the children to be with each parent, which can be complicated, depending on where the parents live. Mobility rights are also an issue because Canadian parents move within Canada and abroad. The ability of a parent to move with the children in such a way that interferes with the other parent's time with the children is very restricted in Canada. Another issue that involves careful balancing between households is managing the religious practices of the children. This can include a parent insisting on a particular religious upbringing or, alternatively, a parent insisting on no religious training in their upbringing.

The bottom line is that if you are married and have children or have blended children into a new family and you then separate and you are unable to agree on a post-separation custody-access arrangement, a court will examine the best interests of your children and then grant one parent custody, the other parent access, or use one of the other options of joint custody, shared parenting or parallel parenting and apportion rights and responsibilities for the children accordingly. (For more information on this topic, see my book *Surviving Your Divorce: A Guide to Canadian Family Law* (4th ed) Wiley & Sons, Chapter 7.)

Financial Support

There is a uniform method for the calculation of child support due to the implementation in 1997 of the Child Support Guidelines. The Child Support Guidelines have the force of federal and provincial law by virtue of some amendments to the federal *Divorce Act* and provincial family laws. Related amendments were also made at the same time to the *Income Tax Act*. The Child Support Guidelines were updated in May of 2006 and the impact of the guidelines has been to bring a great deal of predictability to the area of family law. These guidelines ensure fairness and consistency in the amount of child support. They also reduce the likelihood of conflict between parents and lawyers arguing over how much child support is appropriate. The Guidelines provide a faster and less costly way of resolving the issue of child support when families separate. It was also the Guidelines that converted the approach to child support from one of income tax deductibility to net amounts. Once the amount of child support is calculated, it is paid to a recipient parent who does not include it in their income nor does the paying parent deduct it from their income. It is net after-tax dollars flowing from household to household.

The application of the Child Support Guidelines formula involves the use of tables that establish monthly amounts for child support based on the number of children in question and the paying spouses' gross annual income. To use the tables one parent must be the custodial parent or the parent who has primary residence for the children. This would generally mean that the other parent has the children 40 percent or less of the time. In many cases, however, children reside with one parent for at least 65 percent or 70 percent of the time. The access parent may be seeing the children every second weekend and perhaps one overnight visit in alternate weeks. Vacation time and holidays are split equitably between the parents or in such a way that allows the accommodation of their own vacation schedules.

The child support falls into two categories: a base monthly amount of child support and a sharing of special expenses for the children. In the calculation of the base monthly child support, the annual income of the custodial parent is not taken into account. The guidelines focus on the gross annual income of the non-custodial parent. Lawyers have software programs that calculate the amount of support and it is possible to go to the federal Department of Justice website (www.justice.gc.ca/eng/index) and do the calculation online.

Each Province has its own version of the Guidelines for application to provincial support orders. They are designed and tailored to each province's respective standard and cost of living. This means that a person paying child support in Ontario will have a slightly different figure on a monthly basis than a person paying child support in Nova Scotia, even though they may have the same gross annual income.

In applying the Guidelines, six questions are posed:

1. How many children are involved?
2. What is the custody arrangement?
3. What is the annual income of the paying parent?
4. What does the table in the Guidelines set out as the amount?
5. Are there any extraordinary or special expenses for the children?
6. Will there be undue hardship if the Child Support Guidelines are used in the particular circumstances of this case?

An example of the application of the Child Support Guidelines would be as follows: Let's assume that a mother and father have separated and there are three children and that the father earns $81,900 per year. His child support obligation would be $1,541 per month for the three children. (For more detailed information about the calculation of child support, see my book *Surviving Your Divorce: A Guide to Canadian Family Law*, Chapter 7 and the Appendices which contain the Child Support Guidelines.)

The foregoing monthly amount of support, called the base amount of support, is supposed to assist a parent with the cost of housing, clothing, feeding, and meeting the miscellaneous day- to-day expenses of the children. Over and above that base amount, both the custodial and non-custodial parent also contribute to what are called "special or extraordinary expenses" related to the children. They should consult each other prior to incurring these expenses and then divide them in proportion to their annual incomes. So, for example, if a child is a talented figure skater and requires special lessons, and custom skates, and must travel to competitive events, this would likely be considered an expense over and above the base amount incurred each month for that child by the custodial parent. The parents would typically consult with each other, agree on the incurring of the special expense and then divide it in proportion to their annual incomes. There is no fixed list of special expenses because these types of things vary from family to family, but consider some of the following possible special expenses:

- childcare expenses incurred as a result of a custodial parent's employment, illness, disability or education, or training for employment
- that portion of medical and dental insurance premiums attributed to the child
- health-related expenses that exceed insurance reimbursement for the child's treatment for orthotics, professional counseling, social workers, psychiatrists, physiotherapy, speech therapy, hearing aids, glasses and contact lenses
- extraordinary expenses for primary or secondary school education or for any other educational programs that meet the child's particular needs
- expenses for post-secondary education including residence, tuition, books, and even a new computer
- extraordinary expenses for special extracurricular activities such as sports or music
- the most frequent special expense—braces!

These types of expenses are supposed to be reasonable in the context of the particular family. Generally, the higher the level of income, the more extensive the availability of special expenses for the children.

For example, private school might be considered an appropriate special expense for a particular family, if the incomes are high on the other hand, in a Saskatchewan case, the court ruled that piano lessons were too expensive for the particular family in question.

As the parents' incomes go up and down, the amount of child support changes. This is usually calculated on an annual basis. Once income tax returns and Notices of Assessment have been received. It can sometimes be an open question about when the child support should end. If a child turns 18 and is no longer in school, child support will end generally. If a child continues in school, then the child support may continue until that child is in his or her early twenties. If a child has special medical needs or is, for example, suffering from a disability, the child support can continue indefinitely.

One issue that arises in marriages involving blended families is the obligation of a step-parent for child support after the separation. In such cases the court attempts to determine whether a parent has acted as if he or she was the child's parent (called *loco parentis*), even though they are not the biological or adoptive parent. The court will ask questions such as:

- Did this person provide a large part of the financial support necessary for the child?
- Did the person intend to step into the shoes of a parent?
- Was the relationship between the person and the child a continuing one with some permanency?
- Can inferences be drawn from the treatment the child would receive were he or she living with the biological parent?
- Has the person ceased to act as a parent of that child?

The court also looks at such things as the affection between the person and child, the length of time of the association, and whether the child has taken the surname of that step-parent and lives in the same dwelling.

The Child Support Guidelines even deal with such things as split custody (where one child goes to live with one parent and another child goes to live with the other parent), situations where there is more than one parent obligated to pay child support, situations of financial hardship, and situations where the non-custodial parent sees the child more than 40 percent of the time (and the Guidelines don't apply). All of these things have an impact on the calculation of the amount of child support.

The bottom line for child support is that if you separate, the Child Support Guidelines will supply a reliable method of calculating child support, potentially until your children complete university.

WHAT HAPPENS TO PROPERTY THAT WE OWNED BEFORE WE WERE MARRIED?

Each province and territory in Canada has a slightly different method of handling the division of property at the time of separation for legally married couples. Common-law couples have no statutory rights in most Canadian provinces at the time their relationship ends. (For more information about the treatment of common-law couples and the use of cohabitation agreements see my book *Do We Need a Cohabitation Agreement?*)

Although each province and territory has its own separate piece of legislation governing division of property, the overall approach is uniform. As we saw in Chapter 3, marriage is considered to be a partnership and as such the growth of the partnership between the date of marriage and the date of separation is to be allocated fairly between both spouses. Essentially if a legally married couple separates, the law states that a calculation of their respective net worths should be performed as of the day that they separated. Once a determination is made about the respective net worths, the law then allocates the value of assets in such a way to ensure that each spouse leaves the marriage with approximately the same value in property. In this chapter we will be looking at some of the special rules that govern the division of property for legally married couples. Let's begin with a consideration of the word "property."

What Is Property?

Property includes any and all assets owned by either spouse, no matter where those assets are located in the world. In other words, a condo owned in Florida, a time-share in Europe, a plane stored in the United States, and even money in a Swiss bank account all form part of the calculation of net worth at the date of separation.

The Ontario *Family Law Act* sets out a comprehensive definition of property and states that it includes any interest, present or future, vested or contingent, in real or personal property and includes, for example, property over which a spouse has a power of appointment exercisable in favour of himself or herself, property held in trust, an interest in a pension plan that has vested. There are hundreds of cases from coast to coast in Canada that interpret the meaning of "property" in particular situations. Cars, real estate, furniture, jewellery, milk quotas, shares in companies, stock options, golf club memberships, payments made as a part of an employment contract for non-competition, to mention only a few, have all been considered "property" subject to division at the end of a marriage.

Property Owned Before Marriage

In most cases a couple marrying have acquired property and/or debts prior to entering into their marriage. This can be particularly so if the marriage is a second or third: a spouse may have a home that they have salvaged from a previous divorce; they may have an estate that remains after the death of a prior spouse; or they may have simply acquired assets during their life as a single person, including pension plan contributions, homes, recreational property, vehicles, and savings.

In addition, couples acquire liabilities prior to marriage. These may include credit card debt, a mortgage on a property that is owned, loans that must be repaid to family members, student loans, unpaid judgments, unpaid fines, and, in some cases, unpaid income taxes. As an individual enters a marriage, it is possible to calculate their net worth as of the day before they marry. This is done by taking the sum total of their assets and deducting their liabilities. It is important for each spouse to have a clear grasp of their assets and liabilities as of the date of marriage: firstly, because this is essentially what they bring to the partnership, good or bad; secondly, because should the marriage not work out, or should there be a death of a spouse, the calculation of division of property will need to factor in this net worth as of the date of marriage.

In a very basic example, imagine the situation of Erica and David. As of the date of marriage, David has $30,000 in RSPs and $10,000 in credit card debt. His net worth is $20,000. Erica, as she enters the marriage, has a car worth $15,000, outstanding financing on the car of $5,000, a tax-free savings account containing $5,000 and credit card debt of $2,000. Her net worth is $13,000. If Erica and David are married for 10 years and then separate, as of the day that they separate they will receive a credit for the value of property brought into the marriage. It is therefore important for couples to have a firm grasp of the assets and liabilities which they bring into the marriage. As we will see in the upcoming sections, there are exceptions to some of these rules, but as a starting point, understand your net worth as of the date of marriage. You can use the worksheets in the appendices to this book to assist you in tracking that information.

As we saw in Chapter 3, "Your Rights and Responsibilities to Each Other If You Are Married but Do Not Have a Marriage Contract," subject to one major exception (the matrimonial home), there are no restrictions on the use of property owned by a spouse during the course of the relationship. If one spouse owns a car in his or her name alone and they wish to sell it, they are free to do so. If a spouse has RSPs and they wish to cash in those RSPs to pay for a family vacation, they may do so. Each spouse continues to have freedom of action with respect to their assets during the marriage.

Unfortunately, this is also the case with respect to liabilities and each spouse is free to incur liabilities such as credit card debt or unpaid taxes. The exception mentioned in Chapter 3 is the matrimonial home and neither spouse may sell or encumber a matrimonial home without the other spouse's consent. This means that even though a home is registered in the name of the husband alone, he cannot sell that property without his wife's consent. Nor can he increase the amount of financing registered against that property without the wife's consent.

Property Acquired During the Marriage

Over the course of the marriage, each spouse, either individually or jointly with the other spouse, will acquire property: savings and RSPs may be accumulated; pension contributions may accrue; valuable hobbies may be undertaken, such as coin collecting. All property acquired by either or both spouses over the course of the marriage flows into an asset pool which, as of the day that they separate, is subjected to the provincial or territorial formula for division. The calculation of net worth, which I described as occurring as of date of marriage, is repeated as of the date of separation.

Consider Erica and David, who, 10 years after marriage, have accumulated assets as follows:

> David is now a co-owner of a business; he has stock options and an extensive portfolio of investments which he manages on his own. He owns a Harley-Davidson Motorcycle, valued at $50,000 and has a coin collection worth $75,000. He is a member of a golf course that has equity memberships worth $25,000 and he has RSPs totalling $300,000. Unfortunately, David has not paid his income taxes from last year, and is indebted to Revenue Canada in the amount of $250,000. Part of this tax liability is related to capital gains taxes that were incurred on the sale of various assets.
>
> Erica, on the other hand, has accumulated $50,000 in RSPs; she has a vehicle worth $10,000 and a half-interest in a small vintage clothing store. She has credit card debt of $10,000 and owes university tuition of $5,000 as she returned to school a year prior to separation.
>
> David and Erica will calculate their net worth as of the date of separation and they will deduct from that net worth the value of assets that were brought into the marriage to obtain their net net worth as of their date of separation. It is those two figures that will be compared to ensure that David and Erica leave the marriage with a fair division of the assets that were acquired.

The Matrimonial Home

The most important asset that most legally married couples acquire is the matrimonial home. As a result, it is afforded special protection in family law in virtually every province and territory. A matrimonial home includes every property in which a person has an interest and that was ordinarily occupied by the person and his or her spouse as their family residence at the time of separation. The category can include a rental property, a condominium, a property in which the couple have shares rather than title, and part of a farm that is used for residential purposes. As indicated earlier, a matrimonial home may not be sold or encumbered without the permission of both spouses.

Additional special protections with respect to matrimonial homes include the loss of any ability to exclude its value from division (except by marriage contract), even if it is a property owned prior to the marriage, but used as a matrimonial home after the marriage. Consider the situation faced by Alfred and Jennifer. Alfred has been divorced from his first wife for five years. In the settlement of his first divorce, he retained ownership of a home. It is registered in his name alone. He and Jennifer married two years ago and decided to live in Alfred's home after the marriage. Jennifer gave up her apartment and moved in with him within days of the marriage. If the marriage is unsuccessful, Alfred will divide the value of the matrimonial home with Jennifer even though he brought it into the marriage.

Contrast this situation with what would have happened if this property was never used as a matrimonial home by the couple. If Alfred had leased his home and then acquired a new property with Jennifer, the home that he preserved from his first divorce would have never been used as a matrimonial home by him and Jennifer. As such, Alfred would be entitled to exclude the value of that home from division at the time of separation. In addition, if during the course of the marriage Alfred wished to place some financing on that home, he could do so without Jennifer's permission, as it is not a matrimonial home. As you can see, use of a property as a matrimonial home during the course of the marriage has a profound impact on whether that property's value will be shared in the event of separation or the death of a spouse.

An additional protection for the matrimonial home includes the right to possession. As of the date of separation, each spouse is entitled to claim possession of a property that was used as a matrimonial home. This right to claim possession cannot be given away or even surrendered in a marriage contract. This was designed to ensure that both spouses, regardless of ownership of the matrimonial home at the date of separation, would be able to claim an entitlement to stay in the home until they could find other accommodations.

Consider for example the situation of Donna and Rick, married 10 years ago. Donna brought a property into the marriage and it was used as a matrimonial home. Rick signed a marriage contract releasing any right to make a claim against the property in the event of separation or death. At the time of their separation, Rick had evolved into a stay-at-home dad, caring for the couple's children and was effectively unemployed. Donna attempted to force Rick from their home but learned from her lawyer that even though Rick had released his interest in the value of the property, he had the right to claim possession of it until he could obtain alternative accommodations.

In one case, a spouse brought a multi-unit building into the marriage. As a couple they occupied one of the units in the building and rented out the others. When the marriage broke down, the court ruled that the spouse who brought the multi-unit building into the marriage could exclude all of the units that were not used as a matrimonial home from division. The one unit that was used as a matrimonial home, however, was included when the parties equalized their property at date of separation.

Excluded Property

Although as a general rule all property is included in the division at the time of separation, there are certain categories of property that are excluded. These special categories include the following:

1. *Property that was acquired by gift or inheritance from a third person after the date of the marriage.* For example, if the husband inherited an antique car from his uncle or was given the car as a gift by his uncle, its value would not be shared at the time of separation.
2. *Income earned from property that was acquired by gift or inheritance from a third person after the date of marriage:* In this case, if a wife inherited $100,000 from her mother's estate and invested the $100,000 and received income from that investment, the value of the income would not be subject to division at the time of separation.
3. *The damages for personal injuries, nervous shock, mental distress, or loss of guidance, care, and companionship that are a part of the settlement or judgment of the court.* In this situation imagine a husband who has been involved in a catastrophic car accident and received $500,000 in damages for his injuries. If the marriage then broke down, the value of that settlement would not be subject to division.

4. *Proceeds of a policy of life insurance that are payable on the death of the life insured:* In this case, consider the situation where the wife's father passed away naming her as the beneficiary of proceeds of insurance. If the marriage then ended, those would not be subject to division.
5. *Property that spouses have agreed by way of a marriage contract is not to be included in the net family property:* This exclusion allows couples to sign marriage contracts shielding particular pieces of property, or all property if they wish, from division at the time of separation. (And this is why I wrote this book!)

Each of these categories of excluded property is subject to a very important exception—the matrimonial home. If any of these excluded categories include or somehow flow into a matrimonial home, they will lose their special status and will be subject to division.

Consider for example a husband who inherits a home from his mother. If he and his spouse then live in the home as their matrimonial home, it will not be excluded. It will be subject to division at the time of separation. Similarly, if a wife inherits $100,000 from her uncle and uses that money to acquire a matrimonial home in which the family lives, the $100,000 inheritance will not be excluded at the time of separation. If a husband who received damages from an accident used those damages to pay off the mortgage on the matrimonial home, he will lose the exclusion. For this reason, legally married spouses must be aware of the consequences of applying categories of excluded property to matrimonial homes. It can come as a rude shock at the time of separation to find out that while one inheritance was used to pay down the mortgage on the home, the other inheritance received by the other spouse, was placed in a savings account and is not subject to division.

This raises the interesting question of changes in the excluded property.

Tracing Excluded Property

It is possible to trace the value of excluded property from one asset to another during the course of the marriage. Consider for example the situation in which a husband inherits $500,000 from his father.

He takes the $500,000 and places it in a GIC. Two years later he cashes in the GIC and invests the funds which have grown to $525,000, in the stock market. If the marriage then breaks down, the husband may trace the original value of excluded property through the GICs and into the investments, and the investments will continue to be excluded. If the original exclusion can be traced clearly through to a new piece of property or a new asset, it will continue to be exempt from division. It is also important to note that the onus is on the individual spouse claiming the exclusion or the tracing to prove that the asset in question is one that should be excluded or is one that can be traced through to a new asset.

There are exceptions in family law in each of the provinces and territories that allow adjustments in these calculations for such things as very short marriages, unfair outcomes given the way in which assets were acquired or maintained during the relationship, or cases in which one spouse has undermined the financial security of the couple and it would be unfair to divide the property equally given that conduct.

For example, consider the situation faced by Anna and Jay. Throughout their marriage, Anna has been a good saver and investor. As of the date of separation, her net worth is $500,000. Jay, on the other hand, recently became addicted to video lottery gambling and has, over the course of six months, exhausted all his savings through gambling. If the relationship ends, Jay will have no assets for division, but Anna's $500,000 in savings will be on the block. Provincial and territorial law allow for adjustments to ensure that Anna is not penalized by Jay's conduct.

The same would be true in a situation faced by Gary and Cathy. Gary brought a million dollar mortgage-free home into the marriage to Cathy, but after 18 months, it was clear that the marriage would not last. Canadian courts would be reluctant to force Gary to share the entire value of the home, given the very short length of their marriage.

Loans from Family Members

One issue that arises over the course of some marriages is handling loans from family members. In some cases, parents wish to loan money to a child in order to acquire a home. If that home is the matrimonial home after marriage, then there may be challenges in protecting the repayment of that loan to the parents in the event of separation. You will recall that one of the categories of excluded property is property that was acquired by gift or inheritance from a third person after the date of marriage. If a legally married couple were given $100,000 from one of the spouse's parents, that gift will not be excluded from division at the time of separation. This type of gift is a common reason for a couple to begin discussions around the need for a marriage contract.

Similarly, if a couple receives an actual home as a wedding present, in the absence of a marriage contract, the home's value will not be excluded at the time of separation.

In other cases, gifts to the couple or to one of them may be used for other purposes, such as investments in recreational properties, vacations, private school tuitions for children, and so on. Assuming these loans/gifts are properly documented, special protection may be afforded them. If a family wishes, for example, to loan money to their son and/or daughter-in-law, the recommended course is to prepare and sign a promissory note showing the amount of the loan, a rate of interest, and a proposed repayment schedule. This will demonstrate that the loan is genuine and that there is an expectation that it will be repaid. If the couple ultimately separates, the loan will show up in the calculation of their respective net worths and it will be repaid to the parents as originally anticipated.

As can be seen from the foregoing sections, management of property can have its challenges. Spouses who wish to protect particular pieces of property, such as homes, particular classes of property, such as business assets or investments, or gifts, such as money from family members, the recommended course is to identify property in a marriage contract setting out which property is to be shared and which property is not to be shared. If a marriage contract is not used and the couple separates or one of them dies, provincial or territorial law will apply and the property division will allocate the respective net worth. Unfortunately, that allocation may not be satisfactory to either or both spouses. See Chapter 6, "Marriage Contracts: Creating Your Own Set of Rights and Obligations," and consider how to customize property division through a marriage contract.

WHAT IF ONE OF US NEEDS FINANCIAL SUPPORT AFTER SEPARATION?

When a legal marriage comes to an end, spouses are entitled to claim spousal support from each other. Let's look at the approaches used by Canadian courts.

When making spousal support orders, the court tries to do a number of things:

- recognize any economic advantages or disadvantages to the spouses arising from the relationship or its breakdown
- apportion between the spouses the financial consequences arising from the care of children
- relieve any economic hardship of the spouses arising from the breakdown of the relationship
- promote the economic self-sufficiency of each spouse within a reasonable period of time

In making support orders the court considers certain factors including the condition, means, needs, and other circumstances of each spouse. This will include looking at the length of time the spouses cohabited, the functions performed by the spouses during the cohabitation and any other factors relevant to the support of a spouse.

Spousal support is generally ordered to be paid on a periodic basis (e.g., monthly payment of a fixed sum directly from one spouse to the other). The spouse who receives the spousal support payment must include it in their income and pay tax on it. The spouse who pays the spousal support deducts it on his or her income tax return.

In calculating spousal support, the court focuses on the recipient spouse's needs and the other spouse's ability to pay. Much can depend on the nature of the relationship, but generally a dependent spouse is entitled to a standard of living that is equal to or near what he or she could have expected while married. Entitlement, quantum, and duration will vary from couple to couple.

A recent development with respect to spousal support was the development of the Spousal Support Advisory Guidelines. Technically, these Guidelines are not law in the same sense as the Child Support Guidelines, but they are an attempt to bring some predictability and uniformity to the calculation of spousal support orders across Canada. Some provinces/territories have adopted the Spousal Support Advisory Guidelines (SSAG) more than others. In Ontario, for example, the Spousal Support Advisory Guidelines are, as a result of a decision of the Ontario Court of Appeal, a starting point for the calculation of spousal support in all cases. In order to do a Spousal Support Advisory Guideline calculation, a software program is required. Most family law lawyers now have this software on their computers and use the program to calculate spousal support in one of two scenarios: separating families where there are children and child support is also being paid; separating families where there is no child support.

The SSAG call for information such as the length of the relationship, the age of the spouses, and any special considerations such as their ability to work and contribute to their own support or conversely their inability to do so because of illness. Once the information has been plugged into the Guidelines, two pieces of information are generated, first a range of quantum of support which might be applicable to the case. This range might provide, for example, that spousal support should be paid in the amount of between $5,000 to $7,500 per month. Secondly, the Guidelines will suggest a term for the payment of the support. In the case of a long relationship, say one in excess of 20 years, the spousal support will likely be indefinite. In shorter relationships, the support may only be for a few years at which time it would end.

Spousal support awards are among the most controversial and emotional issues at the time of separation. In some cases the value of the spousal support award exceeds the property that is being divided between the couple. A spousal support order of $5,000 or $6,000 a month for a 10-year period has a value of hundreds of thousands of dollars. For this reason, when couples separate, this issue can increase acrimony. Clients zero in very quickly on whether they have a spousal support obligation, how much that obligation will be on a monthly basis, and when the obligation will end. In this last respect, spousal support obligations do not automatically end when the recipient spouse cohabits with or even marries a new partner. Remarriage or cohabitation may be a set of circumstances that triggers a review of the entitlement or the quantum of spousal support. This, you can well imagine, comes as a painful shock to many separating couples, particularly since Canadians, for the most part, are not aware of the creation of these rights and responsibilities as they marry.

Once again, as it should be clear from previous sections, this potential financial obligation can be managed through the terms of a marriage contract.

WHAT IF WE MOVE AFTER MARRIAGE?

Canadians are mobile, moving from province to province and around the world. Where they ultimately settle is where their legal disputes must be resolved. So, if a couple moves from New Brunswick to Saskatchewan and then separates, or if one of them dies, Saskatchewan law is the law that will govern their legal dispute. It is therefore possible to move from one system of law and set of rights and responsibilities to a completely different set of laws, simply by moving from one province to another. Fortunately, most Canadian provinces and territories have approximately the same approach to the division of property, calculation of spousal support, and custody of children. However, there are nuances in the differences and it is important to consult with a lawyer in the jurisdiction in which you reside to ensure that you understand the way in which provincial or territorial laws will apply to you if you separate.

As we will see in Chapter 6, these issues can easily be addressed in a marriage contract by stipulating which province's or which country's laws and rules will govern the relationship, regardless of where the couple resides.

ARE THERE TIME LIMITS FOR BRINGING A CLAIM?

Custody and access issues are never governed by any time limits. The court will always be prepared to act to protect the best interests of children. Spousal support claims are best advanced within two years of separation (or immediately, if the need has arisen because of the death of a spouse). After two years, a court may still be prepared to consider a spousal support claim, but questions will arise about the reasons for the delay and what had happened to the spouse in the interim. How, for example, did a spouse support him or herself for that period? Was he or she incapable of advancing a claim due to illness? The same is true for property claims. Too long of a delay may undermine the ability to make a claim against the property. A local lawyer should be consulted about time limits on spousal support and property claims in the province or territory in which the couple resides at the time of separation. As a general rule, remember—delay can be deadly to a claim. So act quickly to get advice.

~

Now we know what will happen if you marry and then separate without a marriage contract. Custody of or access to children will be determined on their best interests. Child support will be calculated based on the Child Support Guidelines, which are, in turn, based upon the couple's respective gross annual incomes. Spousal support will be calculated in accordance with the Spousal Support Advisory Guidelines or on a variety of factors that boil down to basically the needs of one spouse and the ability of the other spouse to pay. Property division will depend on the province in which you reside. Spouses will keep property they brought into the relationship and property that is in their name and acquired during the relationship, but they will divide its value pursuant to the provincial or territorial formula for property division. Joint property similarly will be divided in accordance with that formula.

Should problems arise in your relationship, there will be a need to establish the exact date of separation as this will influence the calculation of the division of property. These are the kinds of issues that must be dealt with if a couple does not have a marriage contract. Now let's turn to what happens if one of you is injured, becomes ill, or dies, and a marriage contract is not in place.

5

LEGAL CONSEQUENCES OF MARRYING: RIGHTS AND RESPONSIBILITIES IF ONE OF YOU DIES OR IS INJURED

Many couples must face something even more frightening than separation—the catastrophic injury, illness, and even death of their partner. When these challenges arise, their rights and responsibilities as spouses may be brought into very sharp focus.

As we saw in Chapter 3, in the section What about Wills and Powers of Attorney, couples can address the possibility of these challenges with Powers of Attorney for Personal Care, Powers of Attorney for Property, Wills, and even through a marriage contract. But what if these documents are not in place? What happens when someone gets very sick, is seriously injured, or dies? Here are some scenarios that are more common than you think:

1. Megan and David have been married for four years. They have two children and are living in a home owned in David's name alone. On the weekend, David suffered a head injury while biking and is in a coma. Will Megan be able to make decisions to help David while he is in a coma? What about their home and bank accounts? What about his personal care while in hospital?

2. Elana and Sebastian have been married for six years and live in a home that is registered in Elana's name alone. They have a joint bank account and they run a bed and breakfast together. This morning, while driving to work, Elana was killed in a car accident. Her will, made 10 years ago, leaves everything to her sister. Will Sebastian have any rights to share in Elana's estate? Will her sister get everything?
3. Sean and Valda have been married for 10 years. Sean has children from a previous relationship. He dies without a will. Will Valda be entitled to Sean's estate?
4. Elizabeth and Joel have only been married for a year but they keep all their money in one joint account. Joel died suddenly but left a will that doesn't mention the account. Should Elizabeth keep all the money in the joint account or should Joel's share be turned over to his estate to be shared with other beneficiaries?

These are typical questions faced by legally married couples every day. A note of caution at the outset, though: each province has a slightly different approach to the treatment of legally married couples at the time of the death of a spouse. The examples I use in this chapter are designed to demonstrate what happens in most provinces. So remember, always check with a local lawyer. For now, let's look at each of these challenges.

JOINT PROPERTY

If the legally married couple owns real property jointly and then one of them dies, the deceased's interest in the property is automatically transferred to the surviving spouse. This transfer occurs by virtue of what is called the "rule of survivorship." The surviving spouse does not need to do anything and the deceased's interest in the property does not even pass through or form a part of his or her estate. It is an excellent method for couples to pass on property upon death. If the couple owns a property together, but the title is not held jointly, then it may be held as tenants-in-common. This means that, if either spouse dies, their interest in the property will flow into their estate and be shared by beneficiaries generally, or someone specific if the deceased named a particular person to receive his or her interest in that property.

Similarly, if the property is held as tenants-in-common, and the deceased does not have a will, then an intestacy will apply and all property will flow into the hands of someone appointed by the court to administer the estate. Surviving spouses and other family members will then get in line to see if they share in the estate.

Look again at examples 2 and 3 above. In the case of example 2, Elana's will won't be enforced as her marriage to Sebastian had the effect of revoking the will made 10 years ago. In every province, marriage revokes an existing will unless the will is made in contemplation of the marriage. Because Elana's will is revoked by virtue of her marriage to Sebastian, she has now died intestate. However, if Elana and Sebastian had held real property as joint tenants, Sebastian would have received the home outright regardless of Elana having a will or not. If Sebastian and Elana had held the real property as tenants-in-common, Sebastian would have retained his half of the property and Elana's half would flow into her estate to be administered by someone appointed by the court.

In the case of example 3, Sean died intestate and his legal surviving spouse, Valda, will be entitled to a preferential share of his estate. His children will be entitled to a share of anything left after Valda has received that preferential share. Had Sean and Valda held real property as joint tenants, Valda would receive his half by virtue of the *Rule of Survivorship.*

JOINT ACCOUNTS

In examples 1 and 4, spouses Megan and Elizabeth will be trying to deal with bank accounts. In Megan's case David is in a coma. If he has left a Power of Attorney for Property (naming her), then Megan will have no difficulty making decisions to help him, herself, and the children while he is in a coma. If he has not left a Power of Attorney for Property, then the only money that Megan will be able to access immediately is her own bank account and any funds that may have been held with David in a joint account. If David had complete control of the bank accounts, and they were all in his name, then Megan may have a problem as financial institutions may insist that a Power of Attorney be presented in order to deal with those accounts. If David has left a Power of Attorney for Personal Care, naming Megan, she will have the ability to direct hospitals and other health professionals to deal with David's care. Otherwise, she may be left debating these issues with hospital staff and even other family members.

In the case of Elizabeth (example 4), her problem may be establishing an entitlement to all or even half of the funds in the joint account she held with Joel. Joel left a will so the beneficiaries of Joel's estate will insist that all money in the joint account be returned to his estate and shared by all of his beneficiaries. These beneficiaries may very well include Elizabeth, but the estate trustee will be under pressure to gather up all of Joel's assets including the full balance in the joint account for distribution. Technically, at least in the eyes of Revenue Canada for example, the funds remaining in the account are Elizabeth's. However, if Joel left some evidence of his intention with respect to the funds in this account, then that intention will be determinative of the account's status. Canadian courts have said recently that specific evidence of the deceased's intention with respect to a joint account is important. Even a letter setting out the deceased person's intention (this letter perhaps could be kept with the will or with the power of attorney) will be satisfactory. In the absence of such evidence of intention, the court will be more likely to assume that a surviving wife or child whose name is on a joint account is supposed to receive the funds in the account outright. Despite this assumption though, surviving spouses still end up in arguments with other family members and beneficiaries about the status of these funds.

HAVING A WILL AND NOT HAVING A WILL

If I could snap my fingers and put one thing in place for all couples, it would be that they have a will setting out their intentions with respect to property at the time of their death. Dying intestate creates so much tension, expense, and delay for surviving family members that it is really not fair to burden them with those kinds of issues during a time of grief.

Examples of Common Situations

Let's consider some common situations.

1. The deceased left a will leaving everything to his or her spouse.

In a perfect world, this is the ideal situation. The deceased looked at his or her property, made a plan, and implemented it through a will. We will see in a moment there are some potential problems concerning dependants who are ignored by the deceased in his or her will, but there is no substitute for a well-made will.

2. The deceased left a will leaving everything to a third party (for example his children from a first marriage) and nothing to the surviving spouse.

Let's be honest, there can be tension between children from a first marriage and second spouses. For many children, when they see a parent remarry, they cannot help but feel that the second spouse is, in effect, spending their potential inheritance. In some cases, the second spouse is living in a home that was their parents' home. This type of tension is best addressed through a will that contemplates the needs and interests of children from a first marriage. The point here, however, is that a legally married spouse cannot make a will that leaves nothing to a surviving legal spouse. In this case, the deceased tried to leave his entire estate to his or her children from a first marriage. Each province contains a provision in its family law that allows a surviving legally married spouse to be treated as if the marriage had ended through separation and divorce rather than death. In other words, the surviving legally married spouse will not receive less from the deceased's estate than they would have received had they simply separated.

In Ontario, the *Family Law Act* contains a provision that allows a surviving legally married spouse (not a common-law spouse) to make an election. He or she may either take what has been left to them in the deceased's will, or he or she may elect to be treated as if they had separated the day before the deceased's death. This provision in the law was designed to prevent situations in which the deceased transferred his or her entire net worth to third parties at the time of death.

3. The deceased left no will but has a legally married spouse from whom he or she was not divorced.

In this situation, the surviving legally married spouse will have first entitlement to the estate. An administrator for the estate will need to be appointed and the surviving legally married spouse will be the first in line to be appointed. Any dependant of the deceased (as we will see in an upcoming section) is entitled to make a claim against the deceased's estate for financial assistance.

POWERS OF ATTORNEY FOR PERSONAL CARE AND PROPERTY

For legally married couples, these two documents are just as important as wills. A Power of Attorney for Property is designed to appoint someone to make decisions with respect to property in the event the individual making the power of attorney cannot (e.g., if they are in a coma). Without a power of attorney, minimal decisions can be made on behalf of the incapacitated person. Court ordered authority will be required for anything significant, such as dealing with real estate or other significant assets.

The same is true for a Power of Attorney for Personal Care, which allows an individual appointed to make decisions related to health and general welfare when the person appointing the attorney cannot make the decision for themselves. Spouses who find themselves in emergency situations, when their spouse is unable to make a decision with respect to their property or with respect to their own care, may be frustrated in their attempts to direct financial institutions, health-care providers, and other third parties. Powers of Attorney for Personal Care and Property are therefore essential.

It is for this reason that I urge couples who are considering marriage contracts to use the opportunity to discuss and prepare these other supporting documents.

SUPPORT

I touched on this entitlement in Chapter 4, in the section entitled What if one of us needs financial support? One of the legal consequences that arises upon the death of a spouse is the possibility of other financial dependants of the deceased's spouse stepping forward and making claims against the deceased's estate for support.

Every province and territory permits a surviving spouse to sue the estate of a deceased spouse for support. In Ontario, for example, Section 58 of the *Succession Law Reform Act* provides that when a deceased person (whether he or she died with or without a will) did not make adequate provision for the support of his or her dependants, the court may order adequate provision for that individual out of the estate. Potential dependants include the following:

- a spouse, which includes a common-law spouse or a legally married spouse
- a parent of the deceased, which includes a grandparent or step-parent
- a child of the deceased
- a brother or sister of the deceased

If any individual in the foregoing categories was dependent upon the deceased (in other words, the deceased was providing support to them or was under a legal obligation to provide support to them immediately before his or her death), then they may sue the estate for financial assistance. Unfortunately, this type of claim for some dependants is their last resort when they have been left in financial need by the deceased.

Consider, for example, the situation in which Michael lived in a common-law relationship with Stephanie for five years. The relationship broke down and Michael immediately married Sarah. Within six months of the marriage, though, Michael was killed in a hang-gliding accident. It is possible, as Stephanie was financially dependent on Michael as a result of their common-law relationship, that Stephanie may come forward and make a claim against Michael's estate. The same is true if Michael's parents were financially dependent upon him. Perhaps he was paying their monthly fees for extended care. If his will did not provide financial assistance to them, then they too would be dependent on Michael and in a position to sue his estate.

If Michael had a brother with schizophrenia, to whom Michael loaned money from time to time or perhaps paid his rent, then that brother might also have a claim as a financial dependant against

Michael's estate. All of these claims are possible whether Michael left a will or not.

In addition, there is some pressure to commence such claims for support from estates in a timely way. In Ontario, for example, a claim by a dependant must be launched within six months of the court granting letters probate of the will (in other words, accepting it as a legitimate will), or letters of administration, in the case of an intestacy. This means that a grieving partner or dependant must act quickly. As we will see in the next chapter, "Marriage Contracts: Creating Your Own Set of Rights and Obligations," a couple may set out in a marriage contract their respective rights and obligations during cohabitation or on death, including ownership in or division of property, support obligations, or any other matter related to the settlement of their affairs. This means that marriage contracts are not only of assistance in setting out one's rights and obligations while living together or if there is a separation, but also in the case of death or injury.

The foregoing sections were designed to help you understand the consequences of being married to someone and then being faced with a serious injury to a spouse or even their death. The challenges that emerge can be more easily addressed if the couple has in place wills, powers of attorney, letters of intent with respect to joint accounts, and, as we will see, marriage contracts.

6

MARRIAGE CONTRACTS: CREATING YOUR OWN SET OF RIGHTS AND OBLIGATIONS

AN OVERVIEW OF A MARRIAGE CONTRACT

In the previous chapters we have examined the consequences of marriage, the rights and responsibilities which arise at the point of separation or if one spouse dies. A marriage contract offers a couple an opportunity to say, "We don't think those rights and responsibilities suit our relationship; we want to tailor our own set of rules; we want to avoid possible confusion and arguments."

They may craft this agreement before they marry, before any rights and responsibilities have taken hold (and as we have seen that varies from province to province), or after they marry and the relationship is well underway.

Imagine a contract that provides exactly what you as a couple want in your life, rather than anxiety and uncertainty that can corrode a relationship.

In Chapter 11, "Let's look at a Marriage Contract," I have set out an entire draft marriage contract and annotated numerous provisions to clarify the goal and purpose of a particular word, paragraph, or clause. As we move through the sections of this chapter, you may want to flip to particular sections of an actual agreement to see what a paragraph may look like and how it might be customized for your needs.

Let's start by considering some very basic matters that can and cannot be put in a marriage contract. You need to concentrate on realistic goals. There is little point in putting in a clause that a court will simply ignore at a later date if a question or problem emerges in the relationship.

A marriage contract may contain a couple's agreement on points such as these:

- ownership of property
- use of property
- division of property
- day-to-day operation of the financial and other aspects of the relationship
- support obligations should the relationship change or end
- direction with respect to the education of the children
- direction with respect to the moral training of the children
- any other matter in the settlement of the couple's affairs

A marriage contract may not do any of the following:

- attempt to predetermine custody of or access to children
- limit the responsibility for child support
- make provisions that are considered not to be in the best interests of children
- attempt to waive financial disclosure
- prohibit sexual activity with another person should the relationship end, if that prohibition is a precondition to receiving support or property
- purport to waive the right to possession of a matrimonial home
- attempt to waive the aforesaid restrictions

With those basic guidelines in mind, let's look at some of the typical specific needs that can be addressed in a marriage contract.

Providing for Children

While there will be a little overlap in the following discussion, I want to separate for the moment consideration of the couple's own biological children and children from previous relationships. This doesn't mean that the children will be treated differently day to day while the relationship is underway; certainly, the goal in such families is to truly blend everyone into one happy group. However, the fact remains that blended families face extra challenges because of residential schedules for kids coming and going, and financial obligations related to them.

Biological Children of the Couple

All parents have the same concerns about their children. They worry about their health, their safety, their education, their moral and religious upbringing, and they have views about such things as nutrition and how to discipline children. Even issues, such as the pursuit of careers in sports or music or educational paths, are serious considerations for some families. All of these issues may be addressed in a marriage contract.

Typically couples concentrate on four things:

1. *Education*

Will it be public or private?
Will it be a religious school?

2. *Moral/Religious Considerations*

Primarily, what will the religious upbringing be, if any?

3. *Discipline*

Will there be corporal punishment? Who will be responsible for it?

4. *Career Changes Dictated by the Arrival of Children*

If the children have not yet been born, then little more can be said than setting out wishes, expectations, and intentions with respect to children, if and when they arrive.

It is also important to remember some reality checks such as the availability of sufficient funds to cover private schools. Let's face it, times change and the recent economic troubles saw many families make tough decisions about the affordability of private schools for their children.

This raises another important consideration—the enforceability of such provisions if a spouse "changes his or her mind." Will it cause the relationship to end? Will a couple stay together and consider asking a court to force one of them to honour a commitment to a particular religious upbringing?

Consider, for example, Allan and Diane who had agreed to raise their children as Catholics. Diane later became a Jehovah's Witness and wanted the children to be similarly observant. A disagreement of that magnitude usually undermines the entire relationship and court enforcement of the agreement with respect to religious upbringing is pointless in an intact relationship. However, if the couple separates, the court will find their original commitment to a particular faith very persuasive and, with that initial agreement in mind, will then make a decision that is in the best interests of the children.

The same is true about commitments to bar the use of corporal punishment. A court will not likely intervene in an intact relationship if the parents have a disagreement about how things are set up, but it will again find the original agreement persuasive in a subsequent custody/access determination should the relationship end. (Tip: courts generally don't support the use of corporal punishment.)

The impact of the arrival of children on a career can be profound for both spouses. For example, the mother typically will need to take maternity leave. This may have immediate financial consequences. A father may now have extra financial pressure and responsibilities as the sole breadwinner. He may have an opportunity for paternity leave. How can these changes be addressed?

As we have seen (with very limited exceptions), child support issues cannot be addressed in a marriage contract. Spousal support, however, can be addressed. Let's look at two possible scenarios where the arrival of children, career changes, and spousal support are connected.

A Specific Formula for Childcare When a Career Change Arrives

You will recall from the discussion in Chapter 4, "The Legal Consequences of Marriage: Rights and Responsibilities if You Separate," that in the absence of a marriage contract, and particularly in situations where there are blended families, one spouse's contribution to childcare and household activities can be a source of friction. One way to address this potential problem is to include a clause that specifically compensates the spouse for services in relation to childcare or household services. Consider paragraph 8(c), Compensation for Services, as a possible solution.

Spousal Support, Releases, and Sunset Clauses

In the draft marriage contract provided in Chapter 11, I have provided an example of a blanket release of spousal support for a couple. In other words the couple agrees that in the event the relationship ends, either through separation or one partner dying, neither partner has an entitlement to claim spousal support.

As discussed in Chapter 9, "Signed, Sealed, and Delivered," the court reserves the right to ignore spousal support releases if the outcome would be unconscionable for the spouse who is in need. This review of an entitlement to spousal support vis-à-vis the release, is usually done in the context of a court examining whether the couple anticipated the circumstances that exist at the time of separation. In other words, when they signed the marriage contract and included the spousal support release, things looked rosy and both spouses appeared to be financially independent, but when they actually separated, or one spouse died, the circumstances were dramatically different.

Let's consider this in the context of children and career changes. If a couple have included a blanket spousal support release but then go on to have children, the arrival of those children has an impact on the career of the mother. For example, because she becomes a stay-at-home mom, she effectively runs the household and the children's lives instead of pursuing her once-promising career, and the couple may end up in a situation that was completely unanticipated at the time they included the blanket spousal support release. How can this be addressed?

Many couples include a clause in the marriage contract that has the effect of nullifying the release in the event of the birth of children. This is sometimes referred to as a "Sunset Provision." If no children are born, there should be no impact on the careers of the couple. If there is no impact on their careers, then they should remain economically self-sufficient and responsible for themselves financially. But if, through a change in plans or if accidents happen, the spousal support release is abandoned and the couple uses a different approach. The different approach could be either to simply state that in the event of a subsequent separation or death, the laws of the particular province or territory with respect to spousal support will govern.

Alternatively, a formula could be provided setting spousal support at a fixed level. The latter approach can be problematic as it is difficult to anticipate what would be required. My own recommendation is to simply allow the law of the particular province or territory to govern in the event the spousal support release is not going to be relied upon.

Providing for Your Support

This is an important issue for many couples. As we saw in Chapter 4 (in answer to the question What if one of us needs financial support after separation?) and in the Support section of Chapter 5, marriage comes with the possibility of spousal support obligations. If you separate and one spouse is in financial need and the other spouse has the ability to pay, then spousal support may be ordered. If a spouse dies and the surviving spouse is in financial need, again a claim may be made against the estate for financial support. The approach across Canada has been affected by the arrival of the Spousal Support Advisory Guidelines which provide a formula that divides disposable income between two households depending on the length of the relationship, the age of the parties, and other factors. Essentially, it still comes down to an assessment of one spouse's need and the other spouse's ability to pay, along with the consideration of the lifestyle to which they have been accustomed. For more detailed information about spousal support, see my book *Surviving your Divorce, A Guide to Canadian Family Law*, 4th edition, published by Wiley & Sons, and in particular Chapter 7.

What is appropriate for your case? Legally married couples have three options:

1. a blanket spousal support release
2. a formula for the calculation of spousal support
3. a statement that they will be covered by provincial law at the time of separation or death of a spouse

Let's look at each individually.

Blanket Spousal Support Release

With this approach, the couple is saying to each other that, no matter what happens in their lives, neither one of them will be responsible for spousal support to the other. The wording of such a release needs to be comprehensive. See for example, the topic of Support in Chapter 11, "Let's Look at a Marriage Contract." The language contained in that spousal support release clause has been developed by lawyers and judges as an attempt to bulletproof the possibility of spouses attempting to obtain spousal support relief once released. Ideally, independent legal advice will have been received at the same time to make it even more invulnerable to attack.

However, there are two challenges with such a release. First, it can be difficult to anticipate the future and who may or may not be in need at the time of a future separation or death of a spouse. Secondly, the courts have reserved the right to disregard such releases if the ultimate circumstances of a spouse are unconscionable. Consider for example the possibility of a young couple signing a marriage contract which contains a spousal support release. Many years later, after the arrival of children, and perhaps financial setbacks for the family, a breakdown in the relationship occurs and the wife, faced with a spousal support release, must apply for welfare. The court would have a difficult time enforcing a spousal support release in such circumstances, as clearly the wife's situation had not been anticipated by the couple many years previously.

However, barring truly unfair circumstances, and in particular in the presence of effective independent legal advice, the court will enforce the release. For example, in the case of the Curreys, their marriage contract was signed five years into a stormy marriage that had involved numerous separations, and the couple finally separated 12 years after they signed a marriage contract. That agreement had been drafted by the husband's lawyer and had gone through a number of redrafts that included the wife receiving independent legal advice. At the time the matter finally arrived before a judge, the wife was close to bankruptcy in part because she had been obsessively litigating the case and incurring legal fees. Even though she clearly had a financial need, the Court did not consider those circumstances to be unconscionable and enforced the marriage contract against her.

When considering what the Court might ultimately think of your agreement and whether it includes a spousal support release, keep in mind the words of the Supreme Court of Canada which stated in a 2009 case that "the best way to protect the finality of any negotiated agreement in family law, is to ensure both its procedural and substantive integrity in accordance with the relevant legislative scheme."

In other words, be fair in the way that you negotiate and be fair in terms of the content of your marriage contract.

Develop Your Own Special Formula

As an alternative to a blanket spousal support release that may be subject to a challenge at a later date, some legally married couples develop and use their own spousal support calculation formula. This formula can be related to the respective incomes of the couple; it can be developed on the basis of potential need, or it can simply be the selection of an arbitrary but reasonable figure. For example, consider the case of Craig and Valerie. At the time they began their marriage, Craig earned a salary that was consistently in the $300,000 per annum range. Valerie, on the other hand, earned an income of approximately $60,000 to $70,000 per annum. If they separated, or if Craig died and they did not have a marriage contract dictating some approach to spousal support, then clearly Valerie would likely have a claim for spousal support against Craig or his estate. In their marriage contract, Craig and Valerie acknowledged the differential in their income and stated instead that in the event of separation or Craig's death, and if the relationship lasted more than five years, Craig's obligation for spousal support to Valerie would be to a maximum of $70,000. In other words, if the consequence of the relationship to Valerie was to suffer an income less than $70,000, Craig would make up the difference. If Valerie was earning at least $70,000 at the time of separation, there would be no support.

In addition, when developing such formulas, couples will need to consider the length of the relationship. It is possible, for example, to tie the length of any possible support obligation to the length of the relationship. In other words, if the relationship is two years in length, spousal support, if ordered, will not exceed two years. If the relationship is 10 years in length, spousal support would not exceed a set period. If these formulas are negotiated in good faith and are reasonable and in particular if there has been effective independent legal advice, the court will enforce them.

Agree to be Governed by Provincial Law at the Point of Separation

In some cases a legally married couple develop and sign a marriage contract more out of concern for property issues than support. Rather than try to develop a formula or predict the future, or to hope that a spousal support release will be enforced, the couple agrees to simply be bound by the provincial law of a particular jurisdiction as of the date of separation or death of a spouse. At that point, the couple would ask to have their spousal support obligations calculated in accordance with the law and would agree to be bound by the court's decision in that eventuality.

In this regard, see the upcoming section Dispute Resolution, in which we consider some alternatives to going to court. It may be possible, for example, to participate in a mediation or arbitration through which a reasonable spousal support figure is calculated at the time of separation or the time of death of a spouse. This approach may be advisable in the situation where a spouse has entered the relationship and by doing so, lost the entitlement to spousal support from a previous spouse.

Providing for Death, Injury, or Illness

As we have seen in Chapter 5, Legal Consequences of Marriage: Rights and Responsibilities If One of You Dies or Is Injured, legally married couples faced with these types of challenges, may find some assistance in the use of wills and powers of attorney.

Illness and Injury

At a minimum each spouse must have a Power of Attorney for Personal Care and a Power of Attorney for Property (note that in some provinces these documents have different legal names, such as a "mandate," but the legal effect is the same). Powers of attorney allow an appointed individual to make decisions when the grantor of the power of attorney is unable to make those decisions on his or her own behalf. In the case of a power of attorney for personal care, these decisions may relate to treatment in hospital or extended care. In the case of a Power of Attorney for Property, it allows an appointed individual to make bank deposits, pay bills, and even operate a business on behalf of a person incapable of doing so as a result of injury or illness. I cannot stress enough the importance in today's society of having these documents in place. Medical science has been able to work wonders to keep individuals alive after even the most catastrophic injury. No one expects to be in such a position, but the granting of authority to deal with your care and property, should this happen, can be invaluable. Whether you choose to grant this authority to your spouse is a separate question. In some cases a couple may grant the authority for personal care to their spouse, but the Power of Attorney for Property to a separate individual who has perhaps more experience in dealing with financial issues. Regardless, the individuals who have been given this authority must work cooperatively to ensure first and foremost that your care is provided. The power of attorney is as important as a will and if all planning has gone well, at the end of this exercise, you should have not only a marriage contract but also wills and powers of attorney which work together.

Wills

As we have seen in Chapter 5, a will is of critical importance. If one is not in place, a deceased person is considered to have died intestate and it is necessary for the court to appoint an individual to manage the estate of the deceased individual. This adds not only to the cost and delay surrounding the deceased's property but also to the confusion and distress of his or her family members.. You are doing your survivors a great favour by planning ahead through the use of a will.

Statutory entitlements to a share of property upon the death of a spouse vary from province to province across Canada. Couples cannot take for granted their ability to receive a reasonable share of property in the event of the death of a spouse. They must specifically contemplate what will happen to their property in the event of the death of a spouse. In the draft marriage contract provided in Chapter 11, paragraph 13(f) states that neither spouse will claim any interest in the estate of the other except as specifically provided for in a will that has been made by the deceased spouse, or, in the case of intestacy, as may be provided by the laws of the particular province or territory which governs the death of the spouse. In most Canadian provinces, a surviving spouse will have a property claim on the estate of a deceased partner (the laws governing estates do not provide surviving common-law couples with property rights in every province in Canada. For more information, see my book *Do We need a Cohabitation Agreement?*, published by Wiley & Sons.). In the case of legal marriages, surviving spouses have automatic legal rights to claim a share of an intestate estate. As stated above, paragraph 13(f) states that a surviving spouse will receive only what is provided in a will. The contents of the will may or may not be shared with the other spouse. In a trusting relationship, spouses will do joint estate planning. In the absence of a will, or in the case of a will that leaves nothing to a surviving spouse, paragraph 13(m) requires the heirs, executors, and administrators of a deceased spouse to be bound by the marriage contract and to do all things necessary to carry out the terms of the agreement as may be applicable at the time of the spouse's death.

The net effect of a validly made marriage contract is that it may operate and have the same effect as a will. Consider the situation in which Warren and Bonnie have been married for 20 years. They signed a marriage contract in which Warren set out extensive categories of independent property, as did Bonnie. Warren, however, did not make a will despite Bonnie's repeated efforts to have him do so. When Warren passed away suddenly, Bonnie needed to know the consequences of his death for the property which they used during their married life.

An administrator for the estate of Warren would be appointed and that administrator would look to the marriage contract to see what it provided in terms of Warren's property. The administrator would see that Warren had an extensive category of independent property to which Bonnie had no entitlement. The administrator would look to determine who, under the applicable provincial or territorial law, would be entitled to inherit Warren's property.

If Warren had children from a previous relationship, they would very likely stand first in line to inherit all of Warren's assets as defined as independent property in the marriage contract. In addition, property that Warren held jointly with Bonnie would need to be reconciled and its value divided between Warren's beneficiaries and Bonnie. Perhaps this is what Warren intended. However, if it is not what he intended, Bonnie may certainly be left in an awkward position vis-à-vis Warren's children from a previous relationship. It would have likely been much less expensive and less confusing if Warren had simply made a will stating that, while certain property would be treated as independent in the event of separation, it might be treated as joint property in the event of death.

For example, if Warren and Bonnie occupied a home, Warren may have wished that that home would be treated as independent property if he and Bonnie separated, but Bonnie's sole property if Warren should pass away. These types of consequences need to be contemplated at the time the marriage contract is negotiated and drafted. It may also mean, depending on the length of the relationship and other events such as the arrival of children, that the marriage contract will need a revision and updating as the relationship evolves.

Consider, for example, the usefulness of triggering events that change the impact of the agreement on property depending on the circumstances of the relationship. Warren could exclude a home in a category of independent property unless and until the relationship lasts a certain period of time or children are born. If either of those triggering events occur, Warren and Bonnie's marriage contract could include a provision that the home moves from the category of independent property to the category of shared property and, particularly in the event of his death, becomes the sole property of Bonnie.

You will recall my statement at the outset of this book that a marriage contract should be seen in the context of estate planning. Marriage contracts, powers of attorney, and wills should all work in conjunction.

What About Your Property?

This is probably the most common reason for a couple to need or consider a marriage contract. One or both of them are concerned about the impact of marriage on their property, usually property that one or both of them have owned before the marriage. It can be property that they already own and wish to protect, or it may be property that they will be acquiring in the future and wish to protect.

Each province and territory in Canada provides its own system of property division for legally married couples. As we saw in Chapter 4, these provincial laws provide a formula that attempts to determine the net worth of each spouse. Once the net worth has been determined as of date of separation, the formula tries to allocate the property values to ensure that each spouse leaves the relationship with approximately the same net value in property. There are slight differences in approach from province to province and territory to territory. For couples who do not want the value of their property pooled and divided, there are a number of options available as follows:

- They may shield particular categories of property from division at any time in the future.
- They may create a special scheme for division of their property.
- They may use a combination of a special scheme and sunset provisions.

Let's consider each one.

Shield Particular Categories of Property

In this approach the couple applies their minds specifically to the property which they will bring into the relationship and property that they may acquire while the relationship is under way. Consider for example, the approach taken in the draft agreement provided in Chapter 11. See paragraph 3, Classes of Property to Remain

Separate. In this approach, the parties define what will be considered independent property. That is, property that will remain the sole and exclusive property of the individual who owns it. The agreement acknowledges their ownership at the outset of the relationship and that their ownership shall continue unimpeded throughout the relationship and in the event that the relationship ends through separation or the death of a spouse.

Paragraph 4 of the draft agreement goes on to provide a list of categories which shall be considered independent property and, therefore, not divided. This includes, for example, the property that is set out in Schedules A and B attached to the marriage contract (see Appendices A and B). In the draft agreement, it also provides that any property acquired by a spouse after the date of marriage, but in that spouse's name alone, shall not be divided and will be treated as independent property.

Paragraph 4 as included in the draft agreement is comprehensive and sets out, for example, the possibility of excluding all income, all gifts, all property received as damages, and all property that is inherited. In this approach, the couples apply their minds specifically to categories of property and specifically exclude them from any possibility of sharing.

A consideration that will arise in using this approach is the question of what happens to property that is converted during the course of the marriage. In other words, what if a piece of independent property such as a houseboat is sold and the proceeds from the sale are then invested in a motorcycle. Is the newly acquired property also treated as independent property?

Examine paragraph 10 in the draft agreement provided in Chapter 11. In this paragraph, the parties agree that, if it becomes necessary to divide their property and either party has converted a piece of independent property, then a guide to division of the newly acquired property is set out. In this approach, which is simply an example of dealing with such property, the parties deduct the value of the initial piece of independent property from the value of the newly acquired piece of property and then divide the net equity remaining after such a credit is given to the person who originally owned the piece of independent property. For example, using the houseboat and motorcycle example, if the houseboat was sold for $25,000 and the owner of the houseboat used the proceeds to acquire a motorcycle that, at the time of separation, was valued at $50,000, the owner of the independent property would receive a credit of $25,000 for his or her initial investment and then the parties would divide equally the remaining equity of $25,000, thereby each receiving $12,500.

As I stated earlier, this is simply one approach to dealing with the tracing of the value of independent property into subsequently acquired assets. An alternative approach is to simply exclude the entire value of any subsequently acquired assets. Again, using the example of the houseboat and the motorcycle, the couple could agree that any property acquired with the proceeds of sale of a piece of independent property is entirely excluded. In other words, the $25,000 used from the houseboat to acquire a motorcycle that is ultimately worth $50,000 would result in the entire exclusion of the value of the motorcycle. It is up to the couple to decide which type of approach they would prefer to use.

Create a Special Scheme for Division of Property

Here, the couple states simply that they have developed their own method of dividing property in the event of separation or death. Options include:

1. **A separate property scheme** by which each spouse agrees that they will keep whatever he or she acquired in his or her own name. In other words, if something is registered in one spouse's name, he or she keeps that property. If a piece of property is not registered in any particular spouse's name, for example, furniture, then whoever paid for the asset keeps that asset. This is an approach that keeps the parties entirely separate as to the acquisition and ownership of property. In the event a piece of property is acquired jointly, the presumption is that the property is divided equally between them.
2. **Provincial law property scheme**. This approach is probably best considered as the opposite of the separate property scheme because, in this approach, all property regardless of the way in which it is owned, registered or in which title is held, or how it is paid for is simply divided in accordance with the provincial law.

This type of approach may be more useful for a couple who are not concerned with how their property is divided but are attempting to address something else with the marriage contract, perhaps spousal support or issues related to the children. In this approach the couple simply confirms that they will follow the property division rules of the particular province in which they reside.

3. **An alternative for division of property** is to create categories of property, not unlike the statutory schemes that were provided many years ago in some Provinces. For example, in Ontario, prior to the *Family Law Act*, 1986, couples divided their property into two pools, family assets, and non-family assets. "Family assets" were defined as including such things as the home in which the parties resided, family savings, family furniture, family vehicles, family cottage, and other types of property used by the husband and wife and/or the children. Separate from family assets was a category of non-family assets. This was defined to include businesses, pensions, personal investments, and any other category of property that was specifically identified. In this approach, the couple states that family assets will be divided equally between the couple in the event of separation or the death of a spouse, while non-family assets (which are really the equivalent of the independent property discussed earlier) will not be divided. In using such an approach, though, a couple must be careful to continuously monitor their use of assets. What becomes of a business that, at the time of the agreement, was operated from a traditional office tower downtown but has subsequently moved into a home office, in whose operation the other spouse becomes involved? Will that be a non-family or family asset? It is certainly not impossible to use such a family asset scheme and it may work very well for many couples, but it does mean that the parties must be alert to use of property over time.
4. **The couple uses a combination of approaches.** In the upcoming section, Sunset Provisions and Termination Clauses, we will consider the use of a provision that triggers a different approach. Depending on an event in the context of property division, a couple may agree that one approach to property division will be used unless and until a particular event occurs. Consider, for example,

the possibility of a couple agreeing that they shall be separate as to property unless and until children are born, at which time their approach to property division shall convert to one of the schemes provided by provincial law. In other words, the couple may agree to use two different approaches depending on how the relationship evolves.

The draft agreement set out in Chapter 11, uses an approach that combines the exclusion of independent property and the sharing of jointly acquired property. I included this particular draft as it works well for the majority of couples who seek to protect categories of property but who also wish to share property that they acquire jointly throughout the relationship. The draft agreement also protects against the possibility of spouses unexpectedly acquiring an interest in property because of financial investment, labour, household services, or child-care duties. See for example, paragraph 5 which expressly prohibits the acquisition of an interest in a category of independent property because of a variety of circumstances that may occur during the relationship.

Special comment is needed with respect to gifts. You will note, in paragraph 6 of the draft agreement provided in Chapter 11, that these various approaches to division of property by couples does not need to inhibit the ability of spouses to make gifts or transfers to each other. For example, one spouse wishes to make a gift of the houseboat or motorcycle to the other spouse possible. In other words, the imposition of categories of independent property does not prevent the transfer of a property in that category between the spouses. However, as you will see in paragraph 7 of the draft agreement, to avoid confusion it may be best to cap the value of gifts that do not need to be tracked in writing. Paragraph 7 provides that property of less than $1,000 in value can be given without any written evidence. However, once property that has a value over $1,000 is transferred or gifted to the other spouse, it must be evidenced in writing. This again is to avoid confusion at a later date.

A special comment is required with respect to homes used by legally married couples. Typically, a home owned prior to the wedding will be shielded from division through the use of a marriage contract.

In other words, if a spouse owned a home awarded in a previous divorce, they are often particularly concerned about the possibility of being required to share the value of that property at a later date if the second marriage is not successful or if one spouse dies. As we have seen in the previous paragraphs, it is possible to shield that property as a category known as independent property. You will recall from the discussion in Chapter 4 that matrimonial homes are afforded the highest level of protection in marriages.

Paragraph 13 of the draft marriage contract provides some guidance with respect to household and personal expenses. Note, however, subparagraph (e) dealing with the home. It confirms again that the ownership of the home is independent property and then goes on to explain how expenses related to that home will be divided. Importantly, subparagraph 13(e)(iii) deals with a notice to the spouse who does not have an interest in that property to vacate the property.

Let's consider, for example, the situation of a married couple, William and Libby. William brought a home into the marriage and excluded it from division by characterizing it as independent property in their marriage contract. Unfortunately, after five years of marriage, Libby and William have had difficult times in their relationship and will be separating. Libby, however, is comfortable and does not wish to leave William's home, unless and until she finds suitable accommodations. How long must William wait before Libby vacates his home? He is becoming concerned because of the increasing acrimony between them; he has learned that Libby is now seeing another person and feels awkward when Libby brings that individual into his home. This type of awkward situation is avoided by a paragraph that allows William to give Libby "Notice to Vacate." It also goes on to provide in subparagraph (iv) that during the period of notice, Libby will not entertain anyone in the home, nor will she make any alterations to it. It also provides an extra level of protection for William should the relationship break down and the estate trustee or executor of William's estate needed to obtain vacant possession of William's home in the event that William passes away.

As this can be one of the most important components of a marriage contract, take your time in developing the worksheets and schedules of property as set out in the appendices. Work with your partner to agree in principle on the types of property that will be excluded and the types of property that will be shared. With an open and fair approach, it should be possible to reach an agreement that suits both your interests.

Sunset Provisions and Termination Clauses

It is possible to include provisions in your marriage contract that will bring it or specific provisions in it to an end upon the occurrence of a particular event. For example, Teri and Bruce are going to be married but both of them are uncertain as to how a number of things will unfold:

- Will they both remain in Vancouver, or will one of them be transferred to another province or country?
- Will they be able to live together after each has lived on their own and been independent for many years?
- Will they have children?

Even with all these questions they are willing to give it a try. To deal with some of these concerns, they decide to include a spousal support release in their marriage contract. However, they also agree that if a child is born and one or both of them is required to or chooses to take time out from their career to care for the child, then the spousal support release will not apply. This would mean that, if they later separated, either of them could ask for spousal support to be ordered under the applicable provincial law at that time, or they could decide to include in their marriage contract a set formula for the calculation of spousal support at that time.

Similarly, consider Debbi and Mike who are married and live in a home that was owned by Mike before they were married. They have agreed in their marriage contract that the home will not be shared in the event of a separation. However, they also include a sunset provision that provides for Mike's house to be shared equally in the event the relationship lasts more than 15 years or if a child is born and they reside in the home as a family.

The beauty of a Marriage Contract is the ability to include flexible provisions which can protect the couple's interests but also allow for a different approach later in their relationship.

Managing the Household Budgets and Other Matters

Most of the discussion in this chapter has focused on management of issues that arise upon separation or the death of a spouse. These are not the only challenges or areas that marriage contracts can deal with. Many couples need to consider the operation of their household budget and other matters and choose to use a marriage contract as a way of managing those issues.

Financial concerns are often at the forefront. See, for example, paragraph 13 of the draft marriage contract in Chapter 11, which sets out an approach to dealing with household and personal expenses. These provisions are simply examples. In subparagraph (a), the parties have agreed that they will share equally all costs relating to food, household goods, furniture, and appliance repair. An alternative could be for the parties to acknowledge their different earning powers and divide these expenses instead in proportion to their annual incomes to achieve a more equitable allocation. Alternatively again, the couple could divide specific categories of expenses so that, for example, the husband handles the mortgage, realty taxes, and utilities, while the wife handles food, household requirements, furniture acquisitions, and the like. There are no limits on the variations that can be used in handling these kinds of expenses.

Similarly, consider subparagraph 13(b) which invites the parties to discuss how they will manage their banking for expenses. In this case, the parties have agreed that they will place their respective contributions for family expenses in a joint bank account. An alternative would be for the couple to agree to maintain entirely separate bank account management.

In subparagraph (c) of the draft agreement, the parties have agreed that they will each pay for all other living expenses such as their clothing, holidays, medical, dental, and even prescription drug expenses. Similar provisions are set out with respect to children and, in the event that there are children from a previous relationship, it is possible for couples to agree even on the allocation of child support payments that are received to various expenses related to those children. You will recall from the discussion in Chapter 3, "Your Rights and Responsibilities to Each Other If You Are Married but Do Not Have a Marriage Contract," and in particular the various situations in which many find themselves when they are blending children and when child support and/or spousal support payments are being received from other households. It is my recommendation that these payments or obligations be acknowledged in the marriage contract so that there is no confusion over who is paying for what, particularly as it relates to children.

What other types of things that govern their day-to-day lifestyle may couples need to provide in marriage contracts? Again, the sky is the limit, but consider the following possibilities.

- vacations
- sporting activities
- participation in clubs and other memberships
- acknowledgment of commitments to pay for elderly parents
- completion of education
- acknowledgment of career aspirations and support thereof
- acknowledgment of religious preferences and tolerance thereof
- acknowledgment of special needs children
- acknowledgment of medical issues and special needs for one of the spouses

The list is long and the only caution that I add in terms including provisions that attempt to govern the day-to-day operation of the relationship is the ability to enforce the agreement. There is little point in including a provision that someone will take out the garbage or mow the lawn if enforcement of it is virtually impossible. Instead, I would recommend focusing on matters of genuine importance to the relationship itself.

Conditional Gifts from Third Parties

Some spouses receive gifts from their parents or family members. Perhaps a parent has given the couple a home to live in, but they have also included a condition that the property cannot be sold or mortgaged unless the parents consent. To protect their conditional gift they ask the spouses to sign a marriage contract acknowledging the arrangement. If this is desirable for the couple, they still need to be aware that the parents (or what is known as the "donors of the gift") are automatically considered to be parties to the contract for the purpose of enforcement or amendment of the contract. So, accept such conditional gifts as a part of a marriage contract, but recognize that you have contractual partners—the in-laws.

Contracts Made Outside the Jurisdiction in which a Couple Resides

A marriage contract made in another province or territory, or even another country, can be enforced in other provinces or territories of Canada, provided it meets the proper law for contracts generally and meets the standards of our law for marriage contracts. Support provisions can still be overturned by the courts if unfair. Custody and access agreements will not be enforced if they are deemed to be not in the best interests of the children.

If anyone is thinking that they can simply go out of Canada, sign a marriage contract valid in the country in which it is signed but not in compliance with Canadian law, they should not expect the marriage contract to be enforced here. Our courts will not let a foreign marriage contract do an end run on our rules.

Minors and the Mentally Incapable

Surprisingly, minors can sign marriage contracts but the agreement will be subject to the approval of the court. That approval can be obtained before or after the marriage contract is signed.

Mentally incapable people may also enter into marriage contracts, but their legal guardians will need to approve or sign the contract on their behalf.

Breakup to Makeup: Reconciliation

Marriage contracts may be made under unusual circumstances. Consider, for example, the situation of Rick and Jan who have been married for several years, "off and on." The relationship has had some serious ups and downs, mostly related to uneven work opportunities for both of them. However, they don't want to stop trying to make the relationship work. A marriage contract has been proposed by Rick to deal with the question of their assets and spousal support. Neither one of them wants to be paying support to the other if things don't work out. The issue they confront in drafting the agreement is the question of what happens to the agreement if they do what they always seem to do every couple of years: they break up and then get back together.

The releases contained in the marriage contract and, in particular, the spousal support release will operate if they separate. If they later reconcile, do the contract's terms need to be refreshed or do they still apply if they break up again? What if real estate transactions have occurred after the separation, but before they reconcile? Will those transactions stand? Unfortunately there are no clear answers on questions such as this. It is therefore advisable to deal specifically with the possibility in the agreement by stating that the contract applies to the relationship unless the agreement is revoked or amended and that its terms will not lose any force or effect should they separate and then reconcile and then separate again.

In one case, Mr. and Mrs. Ogilvy had separated and they consulted their lawyers. After receiving some advice, Ms. Ogilvy didn't like the way in which the law would treat her and decided to reconcile with her husband and then wait for a "better time." The court looked at the situation and decided that her decision was "a reconciliation of convenience" and not genuine. The earlier date of separation continued to apply.

Enforcement of the Marriage Contract

We, of course, hope that once the agreement is negotiated and signed, it can simply be filed away with your wills and powers of attorney and forgotten while you lead a happy married life. However, there may come a day when it must be pulled out, dusted off, and considered in the context of a separation, illness, injury, or death of a partner. How is the contract then used? Let's look at two possibilities:

Property Issues

Once a couple separates or one dies and the issue of division of property emerges, the marriage contract is supposed to be used to help clarify the situation. The Schedules A and B that were so meticulously crafted are reviewed to clarify which property was owned when the relationship began and which property is to be treated as independent property and not shared. Ownership of those assets should be clear. The agreement should also provide guidance for the division of property that was acquired during the marriage. However, if a claim is made against an asset of the other spouse, the marriage contract is raised as a defence to the claim.

As you will see in Chapter 11, the terms of the contract are also binding on the heirs, executors, estate trustees, and administrators of a deceased spouse. This means that, if the surviving spouse attempts to make a claim against property that was not intended to be shared, the estate trustee is obliged to enforce the marriage contract to preserve the assets for the correct beneficiaries of the deceased spouse.

Enforcement of an Entitlement to Support or a Release of Support

If the marriage contract contains a blanket release of any entitlement to claim support, it will be used in the same way as the marriage contract was used to protect independent property from claims by a spouse. In other words, the spouse may apply to the court for spousal support and the spouse against whom the claim is made simply files the marriage contract in defence of that claim. If the spouse making the claim cannot convince a court that the spousal support release should be thrown out, then the court will have no choice but to dismiss the claim for spousal support.

Alternatively the marriage contract may contain a provision that comes into force upon separation or death. You will recall from the above section, Providing for Your Support, that a possible scenario which is an alternative to a complete release of spousal support, is to actually provide a fixed amount that will be paid for a fixed period of time to transition a separating spouse in need to a new independent life. Consider, for example, a provision such as this: "In the event of the parties being married less than 48 months and then separating, the husband will pay the wife the sum of $5,000 per month for a period of 12 months, at which time the entitlement to spousal support shall terminate absolutely and be released. No variation of this provision is possible."

If the husband then refused to pay the support that he had agreed to pay, how can the agreement be enforced? Most Canadian provinces contain a provision similar to Ontario's Section 35 of the *Family Law Act*, which provides that the marriage contract may be filed with the court. Once filed, a clause related to support may be enforced as if it was an Order of the Court. This type of enforcement need not be included in the contract itself as it is available by law, but it would be advisable to check with your local lawyer to confirm that a similar provision is available. To be absolutely certain, it may be advisable to include in the marriage contract a provision stating that any agreement with respect to spousal support may be enforced by filing the agreement with the court.

Dispute Resolution

There are a variety of methods available to resolve disputes in family law matters. Traditionally, the primary method has been to go to court to litigate in an adversarial environment. Each side is pitted against the other, trying to poke holes in each other's case and trying to convince a judge that their "version of the truth" is the correct one.

Due to the pain and expense of the court process and the lack of flexibility available to judges (they can only issue a limited number of court orders), alternatives to court have emerged—mediation, arbitration, and collaborative law. Let's look at each briefly.

Mediation

In mediation, a couple facing a family problem such as the interpretation of a provision in a marriage contract may use a skilled third party to assist them in discussing the issue, to reach a mutually satisfactory solution. Instead of having a judge impose a solution, the couple involved design their own. There is no limit on the type of issue suited to mediation. Its approach is different from the adversarial courtroom, because the mediator encourages the couple to look at the problem from different angles and to develop an understanding of each person's needs and interests. The goal is not to develop two competing positions but to determine whether everyone's interests can be met through some creative solution. After all, who is better able to develop such a solution? A judge who is a complete stranger, or the parties to the dispute themselves?

Mediation is voluntary and non-adversarial. It works best when using a skilled, impartial mediator to guide the discussion. Those who have used mediation have commented that it provided them with new negotiation skills that then permitted them to resolve subsequent disagreements on their own. In a nutshell, mediation seems to be faster and less expensive, and it makes people happier with the agreement. This in turn leads to an increased likelihood that the couple will comply with the agreement that was reached. Provincial and territorial laws as well as the *Divorce Act* encourage couples to use mediation to solve problems, particularly those related to children.

Does the use of a mediator exclude the need for a lawyer? In a word, no. The mediator helps a couple work on a solution that is mutually agreeable. It is still advisable to take that solution to a lawyer for an opinion as to whether it is in compliance with the law and in each person's best interests. The mediator will often ask whether the mediation should be "open" or "closed." If the mediation is "open," then statements made in mediation may be admissible later in court. If it is "closed," it is the opposite. Everything said in the discussions is confidential and cannot be repeated later.

At the conclusion of a mediation, the mediator will prepare what's known as a "memorandum of understanding." This memorandum can be taken to the lawyers for an opinion on whether it is in compliance with the law and whether it meets everyone's interests. If it does, then it can be incorporated into an agreement that is signed and the parties are governed by a new contract. Some couples use mediation to negotiate and design the actual marriage contract from the outset.

Arbitration

In an arbitration process, the parties select a private individual, often an experienced lawyer or a retired judge to hear their dispute in private. It is essentially a private court with a private judge and is attractive for a variety of reasons. First of all, it is completely private. The public and the press (if that is a concern) do not have access to your private affairs. It can be significantly faster and more predictable than the public courts which are busy and subject to delays. One of the primary attractions of arbitration in family law is the ability to select an arbitrator who is an expert in the field. In the justice system, judges are regularly rotated and there is no guarantee that the judge who hears your case will be an expert or interested in a family law matter. The arbitration process will go much more quickly if an expert arbitrator has been hired.

The expense of arbitration can be a weakness. The parties are paying usually for two lawyers, now they are paying for a private Judge as well. True, the cost of the arbitrator is being shared by both parties, but it is an additional expense. The only offsetting saving is that, if the process goes more quickly, there may actually be net savings.

There are restrictions in provincial law about the use of arbitration in family law cases. It is now becoming a common requirement for couples to obtain independent legal advice prior to entering into a process with a private judge.

Collaborative Family Law

There's been a great deal of discussion about a new approach to solving family law problems. It is called "collaborative law" and bears a strong resemblance to mediation. Collaborative law is a blend of soft advocacy on behalf of the couple and the use of well-known mediation techniques. The parties do not use a mediator, but rather they and their lawyers enter into an agreement committing themselves to reach a negotiated settlement that is creative and allows them to think outside the box of traditional family law. The clients and the lawyers expressly forego any entitlement to take the matter to court while the negotiations are underway. This means that the threat of stopping the negotiations and going to court over a particular issue is removed. The lawyers promise to the clients that, if the negotiation is unsuccessful and the matter does have to go to court, then the parties will not use those lawyers and will be forced to retain new lawyers. The intention is to keep the people at the table negotiating, rather than dashing off to court. Collaborative law is still in its early days and it is not for everyone, but it is certainly an attractive alternative for couples who are able to work collaboratively and in good faith.

These methods of resolving problems are relevant to couples who are negotiating a marriage contract because it is useful at the outset to contemplate how any disputes will be resolved, should they arise at a later date. For this reason, I recommend including a dispute resolution clause in the marriage contract that states that the parties when confronted with any dispute related to the marriage contract will do as follows:

- attempt to negotiate a solution directly
- negotiate perhaps with the assistance of lawyers to obtain a solution
- use mediation and/or arbitration if appropriate, and only use the courts to litigate as a last resort (providing a method of ensuring a calm and, I hope, an inexpensive approach to solving problems that may arise from time to time)

~

In this chapter, which I hope you have read in conjunction with Chapter 11, I have set out many of the typical issues confronted by couples and demonstrated how a marriage contract may be used to address those issues. The list in this chapter is not intended to be exhaustive; every couple has its unique challenge, problem, or need. Anything is possible within the parameters set out in the above section, "Overview of a Marriage Contract." As long as a provision does not affect custody of or access to children, limit child support, is not contrary to the best interests of a child, attempt to waive disclosure, or violate some of the other restrictions (such as limits on the possession of the matrimonial home), and can be reasonably enforceable, then it can be included in a marriage contract. Just remember: be fair, be open, use the contract to meet your needs and the needs of your children.

In the next chapter we're going to look at a non-legal challenge in framing a marriage contract: "How to have the conversation with your partner in a way that does not get you off on the wrong foot."

7

HAVING "THE CONVERSATION"

A conversation about the need to have a contract can be awkward. That's especially true if you haven't planned the discussion, if you have no purpose or goal in the discussion, if you cannot articulate the reason for the contract, if you have no time to work through the contents of the contract, or if you have sprung the idea of a contract on your partner at the last minute.

On the other hand, if you have a plan, an understanding of why this contract can help the relationship, a purpose that you can articulate, enough time to work on the details, access to legal advice if needed, and if you are prepared to work together, then the conversation can be a marriage strengthener all by itself.

Let's consider some of the things to do and some of the things to avoid when getting ready to have this conversation.

THE "DO'S"

Do make a plan and have a purpose.

Just by reading this book you are well on your way to having a plan for what can and can't be in a contract. Now you need to start putting details that are personal to the two of you into the plan. Take a quick look at Appendix A, My Marriage Contract Worksheet. It will help you get organized and will assist you in preparing your plan. In particular, complete the schedule of assets and liabilities. This will ultimately be attached to your contract and both of you will need to prepare these summary sheets in as much detail as possible.

Gather the documents that support the items referred to in your schedule of assets and liabilities. If you have a student loan, get the paperwork showing the balance owing. If you own a home with a mortgage on it, get the entire file related to your purchase and financing. The lawyer who handled the transaction will have copies of the title documents and mortgage along with any other details. If, for example, your parents loaned or gave you some money for a down payment, this may be shown on the lawyer summary called a Statement of Adjustments. These types of documents are important to show when an asset was acquired, how much it cost, and where the funds came from when the asset was purchased.

As you will see in Chapter 9, "Signed, Sealed, and Delivered," financial disclosure is a very, very important part of preparing an enforceable contract. It is now critical to the validity of these contracts that all assets and liabilities be disclosed as well as their actual values. For example, disclosing that you own a home is not enough; you need its current value and the amount owing on the mortgage.

Do have an answer to the question, "Why do we need a marriage contract?"

Is it because you are concerned about finances? Debts? Is it because you're worried about property you owned before going into the marriage? Is it because you are blending a family and children? Remember, your partner may be completely unaware of the possibility of a contract helping your relationship. Imagine your partner turning to you with a surprised look on his or her face and asking, "Why do we need a contract?" Have a clear answer to that question. For example: "Well, I have done a little research and because we will be living in [or are already living in] my home, which is all I have managed to hang onto from my divorce, we need to be clear about ownership, how we will manage our budget, realty taxes, how we will handle a major renovation, things like that. I think we should spend some time thinking about those things and maybe including them in a contract."

Or: "I have been thinking about the children. We have our work cut out for us blending that gang. We would benefit from spending some time thinking about how all that will work, including financial responsibilities. A contract might help."

Or: "I have been thinking about how we will manage our finances once we are married. Will we need a joint bank account? What about savings? RRSPs? We would benefit from a bit of planning and making sure we are on the same financial page. A contract might help us to do that."

None of the above answers sounds threatening, but they address the key question: "Why do we need a contract?"

Do give yourself enough time.

Procrastination is something that will hurt the negotiation of an amicable contract. If there is a good reason to have a contract then both partners will likely come to the same conclusion given enough time. Remember, if you were thinking about a contract, you may be well ahead of your partner on the subject. He or she will need time to catch up. If you are planning on marriage then I would give myself at least six months time to move from a preliminary conversation about the need for a contract to follow-up meetings, where you gather and share information, to reviewing a draft contract, to making changes, and to consulting lawyers for independent legal advice. Hoping that all those steps can be achieved in a few weeks or few days is unrealistic. You need to give yourself and your partner enough time to work on this contract.

You also need to give yourself lots of time to have the preliminary conversation. You shouldn't start this conversation unless you have time to get into some of the reasoning behind it immediately. I would set aside an hour for even a preliminary discussion.. This conversation is going to take place in a number of instalments and the very first instalment is critical to keeping you on a civil path. Find a quiet place to have the conversation where you will not be interrupted by business, a family, or children. When you raise the subject of the need for a contract, be aware of what's going on in your partner's life. We all lead busy lives and have many commitments and responsibilities. If he or she is in the middle of caring for an ill parent, transitioning to a new job, recovering from a layoff, or just preoccupied with important things in their life, make sure that you initiate this conversation at a time that is sensitive to their needs.

Do use it as an opportunity to discuss the need for wills, powers of attorney, and insurance.

As you have seen from previous chapters, there is a lot more to marriage these days than simply moving in under the same roof. As people blend families and take responsibility for each other moving forward in their relationship, there are many other issues that need to be addressed. Everyone needs a will to deal with their estate. Powers of Attorney for Personal Care and for Property can make life a lot easier if there is a sudden emergency that prevents someone from making decisions about their health and/or their property. In addition, if it is a situation of dependency between two people, or a situation involving children, there may be a need to have a discussion about putting life insurance in place to protect each other and the family. Why not use the opportunity to discuss all of these issues at the same time? A contract can be made to work in conjunction with a person's will and powers of attorney.

Do keep it simple.

In this context, I don't mean just keeping the conversation simple, I also mean making sure that you keep your eye on the ball for the purpose of the contract. There should be one or two justifications for requiring a contract. This should be enough to allow you to agree to continue having a discussion. Don't make the mistake of overwhelming your partner at this first meeting with all of the things you feel need to be set out in the contract. There will be lots of time to incorporate other details as you move forward.

In one case, a couple started their conversation about a contract on the basis that they were blending two families and moving into a home that had been previously owned by one of them. That's more than enough justification for a contract discussion. Unfortunately, they then went on to propose that the contract also micromanage their day-to-day living, including such things as household duties, yard work, and other lifestyle "do's" and "don'ts." The discussion quickly went from looking like a contract to the design of a straightjacket and they took a step back from the marriage. Keep the discussion simple and make sure that the contract solves problems and doesn't create them.

Do be fair and respectful.

As I have mentioned earlier, one person in the couple is usually far ahead of the other in the discussion of the need for a contract. It is a rare thing to hear someone say, "You know I was thinking we needed a contract too." Your partner may need time to come around to the idea and the justification for the contract. That means being patient and being fair, to allow them to digest the information that you are sharing with them.

These discussions can never be based on ultimatums or deadlines. It is one thing to set a timetable for moving forward with the discussion; it is another thing to tell somebody that if you don't hear the answer that you want to hear within seven days then the marriage is off. If someone is in that position they have probably not left themselves enough time to have the discussion properly and they are not being fair or respectful of their partner's need to understand the purpose of the contract.

Let's look at the other side of that conversation—things that can hurt the discussion.

THE "DON'TS"

Don't present your partner with a draft contract.

Take a minute to put yourself in your partner's shoes. You have just been told that your partner wants to sit down and have a conversation about something that is very important. Your partner has set aside some time for a private conversation and there is a sense that it's important. Your partner begins the conversation by saying, "I think we need a contract," and then presents you with a draft contract for your review. What would you think about your partner suddenly presenting you with a draft contract? First, you would think that he or she had been working on that contract for many weeks or months without discussing it with you and that's not a very good start. Secondly, you would begin to wonder what else had been going on without your knowledge and you would feel a little bit suspicious. Thirdly, you would feel that you are being presented with an ultimatum: "Sign this contract, or else." Presenting a draft contract does not produce good feelings.

Don't mention lawyers.

In Chapter 9, "Signed. Sealed. and Delivered," we will be looking at the role of independent legal advice and in Chapter 8 we will be looking at the role of the lawyer in drafting a contract. In your initial conversation and in the early stages of discussing a contract, there is no need to mention that lawyers will be or are involved. In my experience the mention of lawyers being involved immediately gets everyone's back up and creates suspicion. It suggests that the legal wheels are already in motion and sends the message that your partner is way ahead of you in preparation of an important legal document.

Your initial conversations should be about the purpose of a contract, things that it can achieve for both of you, and how it might strengthen your relationship. There is more than enough information in this book for both of you to understand the answers to those questions without any mention of lawyers. Who knows? It may be possible for you to negotiate and conclude your contract without the involvement of lawyers.

Don't rush the discussion.

Again, this is a simple reminder that one of you may be way ahead of the other one in considering this a legal document, and attempting to rush the discussion will only undermine the possibility of some goodwill at the outset.

Don't present a one-sided option.

This contract has to be for the both of you. If the contract that you describe to your partner at the outset is something that is designed solely to protect you, or your property, or your children, it may leave your partner wondering what's in it for them. If the contract is about strengthening the relationship, why is only one half of the relationship mentioned in the option that you describe? Remember, this is to be a fair contract and respectful of both your needs.

Don't blame it on other people.

The need for a contract may very well have been suggested by someone in your family or your legal advisor. For example, perhaps your family loaned you money to buy a home and that is the home in which you will reside as a married couple. If your family is concerned that their loan needs to be protected, that is a good reason to consider a contract. That is quite different from a situation in which you open the discussion about a contract by blaming your family. "My parents will kill me if I don't guarantee them that their loan to me to buy this house is protected. They want me to have a contract." I think you will agree that kind of opening line doesn't sound like a contract designed to strengthen your relationship. Nor would an opening line that sounded like the following: "I met with my lawyer last week to finalize the divorce and he said under no circumstances should you and I marry unless we have a contract."

Blaming your lawyer is never going to be an adequate justification of the need for a contract. A better approach would be as follows: "We are going to be living in our home and the only reason we own it is because my parents loaned me money to assist in buying it. I want to make sure my parents are protected and that you and I understand how we are going to manage our life together in this house. I think a contract might help to make everyone feel more confident. "or" Now that I have the divorce finalized, I think it will be a great time for you and I to talk about how we're going to make sure we have a happy and strong relationship. One of the ways to put our minds at ease is to incorporate some basic financial understandings into a contract, especially around our home. We should also be thinking about wills and powers of attorney to protect ourselves."

All of the above "do's and don'ts" will make your initial conversation, and the subsequent conversations, much easier.

HOW DO YOU HAVE "THE CONVERSATION" IF YOU'RE ALREADY MARRIED?

This will be a different conversation for one very simple reason: what happens if you do not agree about the need for a contract? Let's consider some circumstances which might trigger the need to consider a marriage contract after you are already married.

Kim and John have been married for five years and they have two children, Madison and Jonah. John's family has owned a classic old lodge on a lake for three generations. As John's parents prepare their estate plans, they have discussed transferring the "family cottage" to John immediately, rather than having it dealt with in their wills. This would allow them to deal with tax issues now and not have the value of the cottage form a part of their estates for probate purposes. However, they are worried that the cottage might not pass on from John to their grandchildren, thereby breaking the chain of ownership. What if Kim and John divorced? Would the cottage be at risk? What if it was treated as a matrimonial home at a later date and divided between Kim and John? John's parents have raised this with him, and a marriage contract could solve the problem.

John and Kim need to know their options as they enter into a discussion about handling this asset. If they cannot allay the parents' fears, then they may not receive the cottage. However, if they can, then they will secure an asset for their children and possibly even their grandchildren. Their marriage is a happy one and, whether they address this issue or not, they will continue to be married—but it would be good to take advantage of the offer from John's parents.

A marriage contract in which Kim and John agree that the cottage will not form a part of their "family property" should they separate would solve the problem. In addition, they could prepare mutual wills in which they leave the cottage to their children. A solution that meets everyone's needs is available, provided they approach the issue openly, honestly, patiently, and with full knowledge of the effect it will have on their lives.

You will recall from Chapter 1, "Is This Book for You?," that there is a third scenario in which marriage contracts may be valuable—when a marriage is in trouble and separation is a possibility. Here, we have seen couples use a marriage contract to hold the marriage together under a new set of rules, new assumptions, and even different ownership of property. In other words, they say, "Let's give the relationship a chance but minimize the financial risk through a marriage contract."

With the above examples, I am illustrating the need for understanding your options if you are married and want to have a conversation about a contract. Just because you know the options doesn't mean that you need to place them on the table at the opening of the discussion. Follow the same process of preparing for your meeting. Be able to explain why a contract is required and create options for dealing with your situation. Review all the "do's" and "don'ts" before your meeting and be realistic. If you see rights and responsibilities coming that you do not want, then be prepared to make tough choices.

~

It should be clear by now that how you begin the conversation about a contract is critical. Second chances may be hard to come by but if you remember some basic "do's" and "don'ts" it can be a successful beginning to a conversation that will last throughout your relationship. A good start will lead to a contract, a will, powers of attorney, a budget, financial planning, and enhanced respect and consideration for each other as partners. Let's face it, in a successful marriage you will have a lot to talk about and most of the "do's" and "don'ts" will continue to apply. So, whenever you have to have an important conversation in your relationship, do make a plan and have a purpose, do give yourself enough time, do keep it simple, do be fair and respectful, don't rush, and don't blame others. Good luck with all your conversations as a married couple.

8

THE ROLE OF YOUR LAWYER

In this chapter, I want to examine what some people consider the scariest part of discussing a marriage contract—the prospect of having to hire a lawyer. But let's face it, you may need a lawyer to help with this contract. I say "may need a lawyer" because it is possible to negotiate and sign this type of contract without a lawyer—if you follow the rules and are fair with each other. There is no law in Canada that says independent legal advice (ILA) is mandatory for concluding a marriage contract. However, ILA would be a nice safety net for a number of reasons and in this chapter we will consider the role of a lawyer in these contracts.

WHY DO PEOPLE FEAR HIRING A LAWYER?

In two words—cost and control. Most people fear that once they have hired a lawyer the cost will spiral out of control and that instead of the matter being a civilized and fair discussion between the couple, it will become a war of letters and threats between lawyers. No one wants that kind of risk.

Cost

In some cases, lawyers charge their fees based on a block fee quoted at the outset (e.g., for a total of $3,000 I will do the following service) or they will charge by the hour (e.g., $375.00 an hour times 10 hours equals $3,750.00, plus GST). For lawyers an hour is broken into six-minute increments or .1 of an hour. So, for example, 10 .1s equal 60 minutes. Every time a lawyer does something, from answering a telephone call to preparing a letter, a record (called a "docket") is prepared and recorded in the office computer system or in your file. Most law firms use computerized docketing systems now that track everything, from the length of a telephone call to the time required to prepare an agreement. The lawyer records his or her time and it accumulates until it is time to bill the client. If it takes a lawyer 10 hours to complete the service, he or she may simply multiply the number of hours by their hourly rate, make appropriate adjustments, add GST and disbursements, and—voila—the client gets a bill. It is important in your initial conversation with a lawyer that you understand how fees and disbursements will work with the law firm. This will allow you to manage your cost from the outset. We will be looking at tips for doing so in a moment.

Control

The other fear of lawyers that clients have is loss of control of the conversation that started so beautifully and so diplomatically between the two of you (see Chapter 7, "Having 'The Conversation'"). How can you ensure that the lawyers won't spoil this conversation? Again, this is a concern that must be dealt with from the initial conversation with the lawyers you choose.

Before we look at why you may need a lawyer, how to find the right one, and how to control the lawyer-client relationship, I want to share a little story with you about an unusual case.

A young couple wanted to negotiate a marriage contract. They were getting ready to move into a property she owned. A four-way meeting was arranged between lawyers and clients. She was a young professional, a good saver from a good family, and going places. He was also a young professional and would tell anyone who would listen that he was going places too. His family? Not so good with money. Him? Not so good with money. His personality? In a word, difficult. In any conversation about the marriage contract, this young man was preoccupied with his future, his money, and his career. All of this became very clear during the meeting between lawyers and clients. As I watched the interaction between the clients, I was sure that I could see their future: ongoing battles about money, struggles for control, her continual management of his personality, and unhappiness for both of them. I suggested a break in the meeting and asked her privately, "Are you sure about this relationship?"

"Why?" she asked.

"Is this a life you are ready for? Are you prepared to manage his difficult personality throughout your relationship? We can see from even this preliminary meeting that he is a handful and focused on *his* future rather than *your* future as a couple."

I looked her straight in the eyes and said that, based on my experience and my assessment of their relationship as a couple, I did not want to see her go down that path.

I mention this story because sometimes the lawyer-client relationship is about legal technicalities and preparation of documents, but sometimes there is the benefit of tapping into experience and insight, of having someone on your side who has seen many go before you. The right lawyer is there to provide you with as much guidance as he or she is providing technical services. The young woman called off the marriage and I think she made the right decision.

WHY DO YOU NEED A LAWYER?

Aside from providing the experience and guidance that I just described, when you hire a lawyer you are entering into a special relationship that is unlike any other. The solicitor-client relationship is special in that everything you tell your lawyer must remain confidential. Even a court cannot order a lawyer to divulge information that a client has shared with him or her. This confidentiality is critical to allowing a client to share everything without fear. This means that when you hire a lawyer to assist you with a marriage contract, or any other legal service for that matter, you are free to treat the relationship as an opportunity to share information and explore questions that you may have without fear that it will be divulged.

When you hire a lawyer, one of the first steps that law firms undertake is to search their client list to ensure that there is no conflict of interest. The law firm wants to ensure that they can represent your interest in a way that is not in conflict with another client. For example, if a man and a woman need to negotiate a marriage contract but the law firm involved has been the husband's business lawyers and they have arranged his affairs including financing to purchase property, they cannot represent the woman in the negotiation of the marriage contract; they have a conflict of interest.

Potential conflicts of interest are revealed by a search of the client list. Once it has been cleared for conflicts, the lawyer is free to begin work. The lawyer's primary function is to make sure any contract that is signed achieves goals for you in a cost-effective way. The lawyer's job is to ensure that you understand all of the options that are available, that you understand the advantages and disadvantages of various options, and that you make an informed choice when selecting an option to solve your particular need. It is your lawyer's job to ensure that you understand the consequences of *not* signing an agreement, as much as the consequences of signing one.

WHY DO YOU NEED A LAWYER WITH FAMILY LAW EXPERIENCE?

The lawyer who handled the purchase or sale of your home, who drafted your will, who negotiated your employment contract, is probably not the lawyer who will do your marriage contract. That lawyer may be an excellent source of a referral for a lawyer with family law expertise, but they are not going to be preparing your marriage contract.

As you can tell from the previous chapters, the rights and responsibilities of married couples across Canada vary from province to province and there is a specialized body of law that has accumulated around interpretation of those rights and responsibilities in our courts. You need a lawyer who understands the rights and responsibilities of married spouses. You are therefore looking for a lawyer who is a family law specialist or, if not a specialist, at least someone who devotes a large part of their practice to family law cases. The provincial law societies provide the names of lawyers who have special expertise in family law or who have a practice that is confined to family law. For example, in Ontario there are a number of practitioners who are certified as family law specialists. (See www.lsuc.on.ca.)

In addition to having a lawyer who understands the rights and responsibilities of married spouses, you need a lawyer who is trained in the non-adversarial negotiation of marriage contracts. These lawyers may have even received training in mediation or collaborative family law. These are lawyers who are skilled in "diplomatic" negotiations. They understand that they have the task of protecting your rights, but they also understand the importance of maintaining your relationship.

CHOOSING YOUR LAWYER AND MANAGING THE RELATIONSHIP

Your lawyer is going to ask you to sign a retainer—a contract by which you hire him or her. The retainer will set out the hourly rate of the lawyer, what service they will be delivering on your behalf ("negotiate a marriage contract"), the results that are expected, and an estimate for the amount of time that may be involved. Most good lawyers stay in regular contact with their clients, understand the budget that has been set for the negotiation of the marriage contract and work to bring the marriage contract to a conclusion within that budget. However, there is a provision that I recommend in all retainers, one that is important as a backstop protection for you: if it turns out that the fees and disbursements in the case are going to exceed a fixed-amount cap that has been set in the retainer, you have the option of increasing the cap and going forward, but you remain in control of the cost of the negotiation.

I also recommend to clients that at the outset they spend time getting to know the lawyer. At the initial meeting, treat this as a job interview. You are interviewing someone that you need to hire for an important job. Remember, you are hiring the lawyer not the other way around. I suggest speaking for at least 15 to 20 minutes with three experienced family law lawyers. Don't be shy about telling the lawyer that you only need to meet for a few minutes to discuss your case. Obviously the lawyer is not going to be able to give too much advice based on a short discussion, but you should be able to sense whether the comfort level is there for this important relationship. You will want to ask the lawyer about his or her involvement in the negotiation and the drafting of the contract. You do not want to meet an experienced senior lawyer only to find out that he or she hands the file to a junior lawyer whom you have never met. After 15 minutes you should be able to answer three questions:

1. Do I feel comfortable with this person?
2. Do I respect his or her opinion and experience?
3. Does he or she respect mine?

On the issue of junior lawyers being involved, I am not suggesting for a moment that they cannot provide a service to you as a client. In particular if the senior lawyer can get a junior lawyer to do some of the background work and research at a lower hourly rate, this would be good for the bottom line in your case. However, in terms of the critical parts of your retainer, you, want the lawyer that you have hired to be the one who does the negotiations, reviews the contract with you, and provides the advice about the options available to you.

In the retainer agreements that I have described above, you are hiring a lawyer to provide you with the advantages and disadvantages of various options. At the end of that exercise a draft contract will be presented to you. The lawyer will then be providing you with independent legal advice as to whether you should sign that contract. The lawyer is going to certify at the end of the contract that he or she has reviewed it with you, that you understand your rights and responsibilities, that you have made full financial disclosure, and that you are signing the contract voluntarily. The lawyer certifies the contract. This certification or independent legal advice is considered important if a court later must assess whether this contract should be enforced. Again, independent legal advice is not mandatory but it certainly sends a signal to the court that the contract was negotiated and concluded in a way that meets a certain standard.

BUYING SOME ADVICE, BUT NOT INDEPENDENT LEGAL ADVICE

Not everyone can afford or wishes to have lawyers involved from start to finish in the negotiation of the marriage contract. It is possible to simply buy advice from a lawyer as the negotiation progresses. Many lawyers are happy to meet with an individual to review the options that are available to the individual in the negotiation of the marriage contract and some of the advantages and disadvantages. The client may have prepared a draft marriage contract, assembled financial disclosure, and done some research on their own. It is quite possible to bring that material to an experienced family law lawyer and ask for them to review it and to see if the clients are on the right track. A lawyer in this situation will not provide independent legal advice or certify the marriage contract once it is negotiated and signed, but it is possible to benefit from a lawyer's expertise by hiring them to provide advice from time to time as you negotiate the marriage contract on your own.

USING A MEDIATOR

A mediator is a neutral third party who is trained to assist people in negotiations. The mediator does not impose a decision on the individuals who are negotiating. He or she simply assists them in reaching a consensus. The mediator is neutral. He or she is not biased in favour of one party or the other.

A mediator can be of use in the negotiation of a marriage contract. Many family law lawyers are trained as mediators and it is possible to retain a family law lawyer/mediator to assist in the negotiations. This mediator will not be providing legal advice to either party but may simply assist the couple in generating options that can be incorporated into the marriage contract.

The family law lawyer/mediator may be of use where the issues concern property and finances as well as spousal support. Mediators who are trained as social workers, psychologists, or other non-lawyer professionals can be of assistance in the negotiation of issues concerning children.

The mediator will meet with you from time to time to discuss the options and to reach a consensus. At the end of the mediation, the mediator will provide a memorandum of understanding. That memorandum is then used to draft a marriage contract. At that stage the couple can decide whether they wish to have independent legal advice about the contract they negotiated with the mediator.

~

Finding the right lawyer, whether to provide you with independent legal advice or simply to provide you with legal advice from time to time while you negotiate yourself, is a critical step in moving the discussions forward in an amicable way that achieves the contract you both seek.

9

SIGNED, SEALED, AND DELIVERED

The way in which a marriage contract is made is very important. The provincial and territorial family laws stipulate that marriage contracts must have three key elements. In addition, the way in which the contract is negotiated and the circumstances under which it is signed are also critical to concluding an enforceable agreement. Let's consider these elements.

THE THREE "MUST-DO'S"

1. The contract must be in writing.

A marriage contract cannot be verbal or oral. It is common for couples to discuss some of what they would consider to be guidelines or understandings for their relationship. If they choose to honour these understandings should the relationship break down, then there will be no dispute. However, that is rarely the case. More often than not, the understanding has been forgotten, misunderstood, or one person simply does not wish to honour that understanding anymore. Hence, the provision in provincial law that the agreements must be written. There is less likelihood of a disagreement if everything is written down, even if it is merely handwritten.

A good example of the need for a written agreement is the treatment of the *mahr* that is entered into before a Muslim marriage. It is a verbal agreement entered into before the wedding as a form of marriage contract. A number of Canadian family law cases have considered this verbal religious tradition and found it unenforceable as a marriage contract under Canadian law. When I say that the agreement must be in writing, that does not mean pages and pages; in one Alberta case the agreement was all of two lines, but it captured the intention of the parties and it was enforceable.

2. Both parties to the contract must sign it.

You will see from the example in Chapter 11 that the contract is signed on the last page. Lawyers will often have the parties to the contract initial each page as well as any changes that are made at the last minute. Uninitialed changes are unenforceable. This prevents any argument later about whether the page is an original or whether the handwritten change was agreed to by both parties. Would you believe that someone actually tried to switch pages after an agreement had been signed? So now, as a precaution, lawyers always initial each page to mark them as a part of the final agreement.

There is no requirement that the marriage contract be signed at the same time by each of the parties. More often than not, one party signs one day and then it is sent to the other side for review and the other party, if in agreement, then signs it. This can be relevant to the effective date of the contract. Most marriage contracts contain a paragraph which states that the agreement is effective the day upon which the last party signs it. This means that when a party signs the contract, they should write the date beside their signature. The cover page for the contract should also have a date on it. In this regard, see the example in Chapter 11.

People sometimes ask lawyers at the time of signing their agreement, "How shall I sign it; should I use my regular signature?" I think what they really mean is, "Do I need to write my signature out exactly the way the name is typed in the agreement?" The answer is no; you should simply use your regular signature the same way in which you would sign a cheque or the back of your credit card.

3. Signatures must be witnessed.

A third party is needed to witness the signatures. Canadian courts have rejected agreements where the parties have witnessed each other's signatures. It is therefore advisable to have a separate witness for each signature, although one person can witness both signatures if absolutely necessary. The witness should also print their name and address under the signature. If they need to be located at a later date to verify their signature, it makes it easy to identify and locate them.

What is the purpose of the witness? They simply attest to the fact that the signature beside theirs is the signature of the person named in the contract. Ideally, if a stranger is asked to be a witness, then the person signing the contract should produce some identification to the witness to prove their identity and that it is indeed their contract. The witness is not vouching for any of the contents of the agreement, and there is no need for them to review its contents prior to being a witness. The witness is not warranting that the person understands the agreement, or that they are even signing it voluntarily. They are simply saying, "I saw Mr. or Ms. ____ sign this agreement. The witness must also be present when the person signs the agreement. They cannot be presented with the signed contract and told, for example, "Oh, Erika signed this 30 minutes ago and had to leave, but you know it's her signature." This applies even if the witness knows that Erika signed it and knows that this is her signature. Since both people must be present at the time of signing and witnessing, the signature that is being witnessed must be an original. It cannot be a photocopy or fax.

The only exception to this rule that I have encountered is a British Columbia case where the wife did not sign the agreement at the same time as the witness, but then abided by the terms of the agreement for a period of time. In that case, the court felt it could enforce the terms of the agreement even though there was a defective signing of it. I don't think that we can rely on that case to protect improper witnessing of a contract, so follow the rules.

Resist the temptation to witness each other's signatures. In some cases this has been referred to as a "kitchen table agreement." The husband and the wife reach an understanding about the contents of the marriage contract and simply sign their own document witnessing each other's signatures. The Court takes a dim view of this approach and would likely set aside such an agreement if challenged by one party.

OBTAIN INDEPENDENT LEGAL ADVICE

In Chapter 8, we looked at the role of the lawyer in negotiating and signing a marriage contract. Here I simply want to remind you that there is no law which requires Canadians to get a lawyer to sign off on a marriage contract. So why are lawyers involved and what do they bring to the discussion?

For many years it was simply to make sure that the technical requirements were met, but as you can see from the foregoing paragraphs, those requirements are very straightforward: written, signed, and witnessed. Experienced lawyers will probe the financial disclosure made by each party to make sure a full picture is available to their client. We saw in Chapter 8 that a lawyer's experience can have quite an impact in terms of whether this contract is personally good for the client. In other words, the lawyer can probe the client himself or herself. The lawyer can ask questions that can be answered confidentially when the client is away from family members, their spouse, or friends who may be giving them advice: "Do you want this agreement?"; "Do you understand what you are doing?"; "Do you understand the implications in, say, 10 years if you are, for example, signing a spousal support release?"; "Are you satisfied with this?"; "What if there are children born?"; "What if you lose your job?"; "Are you being pressured?" A lawyer can scratch at the surface to make sure that what lies beneath is true consent.

Involving a lawyer adds an extra layer of protection to the integrity of the agreement. A lawyer's job is much more than simply ensuring that it is written, signed, and witnessed. When the lawyer provides independent legal advice, he or she attaches a Certificate of Independent Legal Advice to the agreement verifying their work (see the precedent marriage contract in Chapter 11). This certificate is a lawyer's statement that he or she took the client through the agreement, that the client understands the nature and consequences of the contract, that the client understands its purpose and is signing it voluntarily, that he or she is not being pressured, hoodwinked, tricked, or bamboozled in any way, and that the agreement appears to be fair for the client. That is what a good lawyer brings to the negotiation of a marriage contract.

If a court is asked years later to throw out the marriage contract, one of the first questions asked will be "Was there independent legal advice?" This does not mean that the court will not automatically uphold every marriage contract simply because the lawyer gave independent legal advice, but any lawyer trying to challenge a marriage contract will have a tougher job if there has been good independent legal advice provided. We will see in the next section of this chapter that sometimes even the independent legal advice can be defective. However, if the lawyer who gave the independent legal advice is particularly well known in a community as an experienced and respected family law lawyer, then a challenge to the agreement is much less likely.

I have participated in meetings where a marriage contract was being reviewed by lawyers with a view to challenging it. When it was revealed that a particularly well respected lawyer had given the independent legal advice, the lawyers reviewing the contract said in unison "Oh, it will never get thrown out!" End of discussion.

At the other end of the spectrum there are cases where one lawyer prepared the agreement in full and sent it to another lawyer for review. The lawyer who reviewed it barely spent any time with the client or analyzing the agreement. Later, when the marriage contract was challenged, the judge called the independent legal advice "perfunctory at best." That contract was thrown out even though there was independent legal advice.

In one New Brunswick case, the judge who examined the circumstances under which the agreement was signed felt the legal advice was not adequate enough to overcome the wife's vulnerability and threw out the agreement. So as you can see, a lawyer's independent legal advice is not a bulletproof guarantee that the agreement will be upheld. However, done in the right way, with the right lawyer, it is a definite layer of protection if it is not just legal advice but *effective* legal advice.

DOING IT YOURSELF

Given the foregoing discussion, why not try and do the agreement yourself? As you can see the technical requirements are straightforward. Yes, disclosure is of critical importance, but if you can assemble a full asset-and-liability picture and lay out all your financial cards on the table, it should not be an issue. You could even meet with a lawyer for a little advice just to make sure you are on the right track.

If you decide to do it yourself, what could possibly go wrong? Let's look at what some people did and how they ruined their marriage contracts. I'm sharing the following information with you not to discourage you from trying to design your own marriage contract, but to help you avoid some of the mistakes that others made. It is helpful to learn from their experiences.

How to Ruin Your Marriage Contract

Before we examine some of the ways in which marriage contracts have been ruined, let's consider for a moment the context in which these agreements come under scrutiny. The two most common contexts are when, if the relationship has ended and a dispute has arisen about property, children, or support, one party will wish to rely on the marriage contract (after all that's why it was drafted and signed) but the other party, for whatever reason, thinks the contract should not apply. The other common context is in a situation where one spouse has passed away and a dispute over property or support has arisen in the context of interpreting their estate.

A typical example would be Jillian and Michael. They have been married for 10 years, but have split up over a dispute about children. Jillian thought they were going to start a family, but Michael ultimately decided against it. They had signed a marriage contract that they had drafted themselves. Each, it was agreed, would keep their own property as it was brought into the relationship and as it was acquired during the relationship. There would be no spousal support if they separated. It seemed like a good idea at the time because they were both financially independent, but now Jillian is out of work because they moved to a small town for Michael's new position with a mining company. Jillian has only been able to get work as a substitute teacher

When they arrived in the town, they bought a house but it is registered in Michael's name only as he was the one who put down the deposit. Jillian has consulted a lawyer and he suggests that the marriage contract be scrutinized to see if there are any grounds for setting it aside. My point here is that the contracts are attacked in unpleasant circumstances when the parties' needs are different. Memories change, attitudes are different, feelings may be hurt, people are often angry. All of this could be just as true if in the above example Michael had died without a will or perhaps had left everything in a will to someone other than Jillian. The feelings could be intense and her needs very great in a small town with no way to support herself. Jillian's lawyer, after reviewing the technical requirements around the execution of the marriage contract, would review the typical grounds for attacking it. Let's look at those typical grounds.

Someone didn't make full financial disclosure.

In order for the two people affected by this contract to be genuinely and fairly entering into it, everything must be on the table. They must know everything about each other's financial situation—good and bad. They must know all of the other person's assets, the value of those assets and the extent of that person's liabilities. When a court is asked at a later date to assess the fairness of a contract, the judge starts with the adequacy of financial disclosure. In Ontario, Section 56(4) of the Family Law Act states: "56. (4) A Court may set aside a domestic contract or a provision in it, if a party failed to disclose to the other significant assets or significant debts or other liabilities existing when the domestic contract was made."

This idea of disclosure was brought into dramatic focus in a case called *LeVan v. LeVan*. Let's look at the situation they encountered. The LeVan marriage lasted only seven years and when they separated in October of 2003, she was 42 years old and he was 44. They had two children who were six and eight as of the date of separation. Ms. LeVan had an Honours BA in psychology and a teacher's certificate; Mr. LeVan, on the other hand, had a diploma in business marketing. Once the children were born, Ms. LeVan became a stay-at-home mom and Mr. LeVan, along with other members of his family, owned the majority of shares in a company called Westcast Industries Inc., which was the largest manufacturer of exhaust manifolds in the world and a publicly traded company. At the time of the marriage in 1996, Ms. LeVan was earning approximately $13,000 a year and Mr. LeVan $52,000.

Mr. LeVan's father had built Westcast into the world's largest supplier of auto parts and he and his wife, Mr. LeVan's mother, along with help from corporate and financial advisors had created a complex corporate structure that included several companies and a family trust. Mr. LeVan's father wanted to protect his son's shares in Westcast in the hope that he and his wife and their four children, including Mr. LeVan, would always maintain control of Westcast.

It was clear from the outset that Ms. LeVan was aware that she would be asked to sign a marriage contract. Her evidence at trial was that even before they got engaged, her husband told her that his family would require her to sign a marriage contract to exclude any interest in the Westcast shares. It was even discussed at the family dinner table with Mr. LeVan's parents. Mr. LeVan's father took the initiative and contacted a lawyer to prepare a draft marriage contract dealing with spousal support and protection of the shares in Westcast. Mr. LeVan ended up meeting with a lawyer at a large Toronto law firm and a draft marriage contract was completed. Ms. LeVan hired a lawyer who was a general practitioner in a small town in Ontario. That lawyer estimated that he spent about 40 to 50 percent of his practice in the area of family law.

Attached to the draft marriage contract were schedules that set out a list of significant assets and significant debts. It disclosed Mr. LeVan's net worth as being "$80,000 plus LeVan family companies' interest." No values were inserted for such things as his RRSPs, bank accounts, or the values in the LeVan companies. The lawyer for Mr. LeVan, when she was called as a witness at the trial, acknowledged that it was essential that the other side know Mr. LeVan's actual income and actual net worth, but she did not provide that information to the wife's lawyer other than as set out in Schedule A attached to the draft agreement. She herself did not have a full grasp of Mr. LeVan's net worth which, it turns out, was approximately $14 million. By the time of separation, Mr. LeVan was worth $30 million and Ms. LeVan had signed a marriage contract releasing any interest in those assets and releasing any entitlement to spousal support. She did so by signing a marriage contract less than a month before the wedding having been told that if she did not sign the contract there would be no wedding.

To make matters more complicated, the wife changed lawyers prior to signing the agreement. When her first lawyer attempted to obtain more financial disclosure, he was rebuffed; when he gave advice to Ms. LeVan and made enquiries of the husband's lawyer for further disclosure, Mr. Levan's lawyer told her client that "she did not think the wife's lawyer knew what he was doing." When Mr. Levan told his wife that her lawyer was "an idiot" and that he was incompetent, the wife was driven to find a new lawyer. Guess what? The new lawyer to whom she was referred had acted for the husband's lawyer in her own divorce a few months earlier.

The wedding was now only a week away and the pressure was on to sign a contract. The wife's second lawyer did not request any further disclosure and met with the wife for approximately one hour. Some minor amendments were requested which were considered inconsequential by the husband's lawyer; the contract was quickly signed and the wife, under considerable pressure, two days before the wedding, still felt that there would be no wedding without a marriage contract being signed.

When the parties later separated and the wife learned the consequence, her new lawyer suggested that she ask the court to throw out the agreement because there was inadequate financial disclosure and the advice that she had received from her previous two lawyers was not effective independent legal advice.

In the *LeVan* decision, the Trial Judge threw out the marriage contract, both as it related to support and division of assets, and made an award in the favour of the wife in the amount of $5.3 million, not quite what was expected by these people, particularly Mr. LeVan and his parents.

In cases involving valuable or extensive assets, the need for financial disclosure, particularly after the *LeVan* decision, has resulted in lawyers exchanging thick briefs of documents with copies of supporting ownership materials, valuations, appraisals, and other forms of backup documentation for all assets and liabilities of each party. Income disclosure includes copies of income tax returns and backup documents for all sources of income. Accountants are sometimes involved to explain the corporate holdings of the parties. This disclosure, before signing, must also be mindful of what may happen in the future to the people involved: How old are they? When will they retire? What are their career expectations? Will there be children? Will someone move their residence to join the relationship? Will one party move their children from, say, Toronto to Vancouver? How will they be supported? And so on.

Many, many questions are asked as a part of proper financial disclosure. You will see in the sample marriage contract provided in Chapter 11, that the parties warrant to each other that they have made full disclosure to each other and that they are each satisfied with the disclosure. Hiding an asset, overvaluing an asset, undervaluing an asset, or not being open and honest about significant assets and liabilities, may well provide an excuse to invalidate the entire marriage contract at a later date.

In most cases, though, the couple may have modest assets, a home, a recreational property, vehicles, some retirement savings, a pension, furniture, and so on. A forensic audit of values and liabilities would be disproportionate to the value of the assets and liabilities in question. In such cases, disclosure is made by the parties and an opportunity to investigate further is presented. If the people are satisfied with the information and trust each other, they may simply attach to the marriage contract two schedules of assets and liabilities disclosing each other's net worth and income. In the agreement they warrant to each other that the disclosure has been adequate and that they accept it without further investigation.

Someone didn't understand the nature and consequences of the contract.

For a contract to be valid, the person signing it must understand the character of the document as well as the impact that it's going to have on their life. There is a strong connection between obtaining independent legal advice and understanding the nature and consequences of the contract. As I mentioned earlier, this is often what a lawyer brings to the table. The lawyer and client will spend a good deal of time going through a list of "what ifs." What if you have children? What if you lose your job? What if you move? What if someone dies? What if you become sick? The lawyer and client review the impact of the contract in each set of circumstances. By reviewing the details, the client comes to appreciate exactly what the impact of the contract will be.

Returning to the LeVan case, Ms. LeVan was surprised to learn, after separation, that not only had she excluded an interest in the value of Mr. LeVan's shares as of the date of marriage, but she had also excluded any interest in the growth in the value of those shares over the course of the marriage. Proper legal advice would have disclosed this important consequence of the contract. As you can see there is a strong relationship between independent legal advice and financial disclosure. Is it possible for someone to understand the nature and consequences of a contract if they do not have adequate financial disclosure? Probably not. Mr. LeVan was relying on the fact that his wife-to-be knew all along that she would be excluded from having any interest in his family's business. After all, what more did she need to know? Whether he was worth $14 million or $30 million at the time of marriage, she would have signed the same agreement. Reliance on that kind of understanding of the nature and consequences of the contract was not good enough for the judge in LeVan and shouldn't be good enough for you in doing your marriage contract.

Someone made a misrepresentation about the contract.

A misrepresentation is a statement that is untrue about the factual basis for requiring a marriage contract or, similarly, not revealing a fact that is important to a person's understanding of the requirement for a contract.

Consider, for example, the situation in which James and Bobbi prepare to marry. If James told Bobbi that a marriage contract was required because the bank would not loan him money for his business without a marriage contract that excluded his wife from having any interest in the company, then this is an inaccurate reason for Bobbi to sign. For James to tell her that a bank requires her to sign the agreement is a misrepresentation. Bobbi has relied on that essential fact in agreeing to sign the contract. If they later separate and that misrepresentation is disclosed, a court will have an excellent reason to throw out the contract. In a way, misrepresentation is connected to understanding the nature and consequences of the contract. Can someone understand what a contract is going to do if the very basis for the need for a contract has been misrepresented to them? Probably not.

Someone made a mistake.

This is similar to a misrepresentation but the mistake need not be the fault of a party to the agreement. For example, if a spouse was under the mistaken impression that a marriage contract had to be signed in order to immigrate to Canada, which is not the case, then the basis for them signing the agreement is mistaken. The mistake, whether honest or induced, is a belief that a fact is true when it is not. If such a mistaken belief comes to light, the court will have an excellent excuse to interfere with the contract and perhaps set it aside.

Someone was under undue influence or duress.

The family law of each province and territory provides that a Court may set aside a marriage contract, or even a provision in a marriage contract, if the contract or the provision is not in accordance with the general law of contract. This means that all of the other reasons for attacking contracts can be employed against a marriage contract.

A typical ground for attacking a contract is that the person who signed it did not do so willingly. In other words, they were forced or coerced into signing the agreement. It doesn't need to be as dramatic as the infamous Godfather scene in which "someone made him an offer he couldn't refuse"; it can, in fact, be quite subtle. For example, in one case in Canada where one spouse relied upon the other for all business and financial decisions, and did so throughout the negotiation of a marriage contract, a court ultimately found that the husband exercised undue influence over the wife by virtue of the dramatic difference in the balance of power between them. Other examples of undue influence or duress include situations similar to that which we saw in the LeVan case where the husband told the wife repeatedly in the days leading up to the wedding that if the marriage contract was not signed there would be no wedding at all. In another case, the person presented with a marriage contract was told that if she did not sign it the family would be extremely angry with her.

When the courts have been asked to look at a situation of alleged undue influence or duress, it has come down to a consideration of the ability of one spouse to dominate the will of the other, whether through manipulation, coercion, or use of power. Imagine for a moment the pressure faced by a young woman who is expecting a child and is then presented with a "take it or leave it" marriage contract: if she signs it, she and the child's father will marry; if she does not sign it, she will be on her own and likely involved in a claim for child support and custody. The court will not enforce marriage contracts entered into under situations that involve violence, threats, intimidation, economic duress, or oppression.

Someone commits a fraud.

This is very similar to a misrepresentation except that, in the case of fraud the person making the misrepresentation has every intention of taking something from the other party to which they are not entitled. Imagine a situation where a husband has a number of documents prepared including real estate transactions, corporate bylaws, and other materials, but slips into the pile of documents to be signed a marriage contract in which the wife transfers all interest in her property to the husband. Similarly, consider the situation that I mentioned earlier where one party tried to change pages in the document after it had been signed. Those are good examples of fraud and a court will obviously throw out any agreement reached under such circumstances.

The contract is unconscionable or unfair.

This is a relatively new development in the area of attacking marriage contracts. In the past, the courts were reluctant to spend too much time evaluating the relative advantages and disadvantages of the deal for the parties involved. The court was generally concerned only with whether the contract met its technical requirements and whether it was valid under the general law of contract. In other words, as long as it was signed properly, and proper disclosure had been made, and no one was acting under duress, then the contract would be enforceable. However, over time as courts were invited in to examine the circumstances under which the contract was signed and whether there was undue influence or duress, it also started to consider whether the deal was fair or not. Unconscionability—which means a situation that is grossly unfair—occurs generally in situations where there is inequality between the people signing the contract and an improvident outcome for one of them. Both must be present; in other words, if there are two parties involved in the negotiation of the contract and they are of equal bargaining power but happen to arrive at a bad deal, the court will not be interested in disturbing that contract. However, if there is an inequality of bargaining power between the two parties and it appears that one party was preying on the other, that they used their advantage to obtain the other party's signature on an improvident contract, then the court will be prepared to intervene.

In the context of unconscionability, the availability of independent legal advice from a lawyer—effective independent legal advice—should be more than enough to overcome problems of unequal bargaining power and improvident deals.

Someone repudiates the contract.

Repudiation of a contract means that a party has refused to abide by the contract. That person's repudiation of it disentitles them from enforcing the contract against the other party. Imagine a situation in which a man and a woman enter into a marriage contract in which the man agrees to support the woman's children and pay for their attendance at private school. On this understanding she moves the children from their schools in one city to the private schools in the city in which the spouse resides. Imagine too that this marriage contract includes a release of any spousal support. If the children are moved and the spouse then refuses to pay for private schooling for the children and the relationship breaks down, a court will not allow the man to enforce the spousal support release against her as he has repudiated the contract. Court cases that have examined situations like this sometimes talk about the occurrence of a "fundamental breach" of the contract. A fundamental breach is one that substantially deprives the innocent party of the entire benefit of the contract into which they entered.

A provision is not in the best interests of the children.

The courts always reserve the right to protect the interest of children. If a provision in a marriage contract is considered to not be in the best interests of the children, or for example is not considered to be in accordance with the Child Support Guidelines, then the court will set aside that provision of the contract and do what it considers to be right for the children. Consider for example a couple who agree when they marry that if the relationship does not work out the maximum amount of income that will be considered in calculating child support under the Child Support Guidelines will be $100,000. If at the time of separation the party who would otherwise be paying child support earns in excess of $100,000, the court will not be bound by the agreement to artificially lower the income.

Onus

Assuming that one party considers themselves to be in a position to attack the marriage contract, they should also be aware of the approach that is taken by a court when a marriage contract is attacked. It is not enough simply to make an allegation, for example, that one suffered from duress. The court has made it clear that, when challenging an agreement, the party who wishes to set it aside must first show that he or she fits within one of the grounds for attacking the agreement. So in the example of duress, the person attacking the marriage contract must convince the court that they were indeed threatened with negative consequences if they did not sign. If the court accepts that evidence, it then goes on to consider a second aspect. The person attacking the agreement must then persuade the court to exercise its discretion to set aside the agreement. The onus is on the person attacking the agreement to convince the court that it should use its discretion to help them.

What is the Supreme Court of Canada's attitude to marriage contracts?

The Supreme Court of Canada, in a case that involved a battle between two lawyers who were married to each other, noted that there were no hard and fast rules about giving deference to one form of contract over another:

> In some cases, marriage contracts ought to be accorded a greater degree of deference than separation agreements.

> Marriage agreements define the parties' expectations from the outset, usually before any rights are vested and before any entitlement arises. Often, perhaps most often, a desire to protect preacquired assets or an anticipated inheritance for children of a previous marriage will be the impetus for such an agreement.

On the other hand, marriage agreements may be accorded less deference because they are anticipatory and may not fairly take into account the financial means, needs, or other circumstances of the parties at the time of a marriage breakdown.

SOME TIPS FOR NEGOTIATING AND DRAFTING MARRIAGE CONTRACTS

- Avoid the appearance that one party is steering the other party to a particular lawyer for Independent Legal Advice. While a spouse may simply be trying to be helpful and trying to speed the process along, to an outside observer it may appear that the advice received was not truly independent. The best advice is simply to ensure that they go to an experienced family law lawyer if they are going for independent legal advice.
- As should be clear from the foregoing section about financial disclosure, make sure the disclosure is complete, accurate, and timely. If the assets and their values involve corporate holdings, for example, provide a flow chart that shows the relationship between the companies. Simply providing a stack of incomprehensible documents will not be considered adequate financial disclosure at a later date.
- Use language that can be understood. There's no need to overcomplicate matters with a lot of legalese and mumbo jumbo. Write it in a language that both parties can understand. It is interesting to note that in the LeVan case discussed earlier, it was clear from the evidence at trial that, not only did the spouses not understand the contract, neither did the lawyers nor some of the valuators who were called as expert witnesses at trial.
- Remember to ensure that each person has adequate time to review the contract, make suggestions, review disclosure, get advice, and

actually feel like they have a hand in the design of this important agreement.

- Avoid negotiating a contract that is simply a blanket waiver of all claims. If you're going to the trouble of negotiating a marriage contract, take the time to tailor the agreement to accomplish something that strengthens the relationship. Simply making blanket waivers may be an invitation at a later date to think of the contract as being unconscionable or unfair to one of the parties.
- Be aware that lawyers are wary of participating in the negotiation of marriage contracts. No one wants to be in the position of the two lawyers for the wife in *LeVan* where they were severely criticized for not having scrutinized the financial disclosure. Often clients will contact the lawyer's office and ask to meet to discuss a marriage contract. Their first question is "Do you have experience in this area?" The second question is "How much will this cost?" In most cases, an experienced lawyer is unable to provide an estimate because he or she has no idea what will be involved. Even after a first meeting with a client, an estimate will be difficult until financial disclosure is produced. As the time involved climbs, the client often balks at the potential bill that is being incurred and pressures the lawyer to speed through their analysis. In many cases a wedding is looming and there is pressure to make sure that the contract is signed. No one wants to spoil the party. The reason I mention this is that lawyers often would rather simply avoid providing independent legal advice on these contracts because the fees that are charged are often out of proportion to the potential liability that is taken on.
- For example, in one Ontario case, the lawyer who represented the husband was sued by the wife on the basis that he did not protect her interests. I know that sounds strange, but it took a Superior Court judge to decide that the lawyer who is negotiating a marriage contract does not owe a duty to protect the opposite side in the family law dispute. In that particular case, when the contract was thrown out it proved costly for the husband. The question that arose was whether the husband's lawyer had an obligation to make sure that the contract was fair to the wife and, in doing so, thereby to protect the husband and the agreement from attack at a later date.

It is a tricky business providing Independent Legal Advice, especially if a contract is set aside by the court and millions of dollars or even hundreds of thousands of dollars suddenly change hands.

~

All of these rules and guidelines for preparation, signing, and negotiation of marriage contracts are designed for a reason. No one wants to see a spouse taken advantage of; no one wants to have contracts signed under circumstances that create confusion and litigation at a later date. Contracts should be clear. They should say what they mean. They should achieve the intentions and goals of the people who sign the contract. Contracts should be fair to both spouses. They should have a purpose. They should strengthen the relationship, not create resentment or anxiety while the relationship is underway. If you keep the overriding goal of fairness in mind, and follow the rules set out above, you will have a much greater chance of your marriage contract surviving a challenge at a later date.

10

SAME-SEX COUPLES

Same-sex couples in Canada now enjoy the same rights and responsibilities as common-law couples and married couples. Their treatment at the time of separation or death of a partner is virtually identical. They may enter into cohabitation agreements and marriage contracts and customize their rights and responsibilities. There are, however, some extra challenges that may be faced by same-sex couples and, in this chapter, we consider those challenges and some options for addressing them.

GETTING MARRIED IS THE EASY PART

Since approximately 2003, same-sex couples have had the right to marry in Canada. I was fortunate to be able to attend the first same-sex marriage in Canada, which occurred in the hallway at a courthouse on University Avenue in Toronto (the wedding occurred in the hallway because no cameras are allowed in courtrooms in Canada, and there were lots of pictures being taken). Marriage for same-sex couples now is the easy part. Divorce, however, in some cases, is not so easy if the couple leaves Canada after the wedding and then later attempts to divorce. Other jurisdictions, notably in the United States, do not recognize the same-sex couple's marriage, so the foreign divorce laws are not available to the couple.

One option for the couple is to include a term in a marriage contract binding them to the laws of a Canadian province, in the event of a separation and divorce. This may assist the couple, should they be forced to return to Canada for a divorce at a later date. The key problem, however, is that our divorce laws require a period of residency prior to the issuance of a divorce application. If the couple has not actually resided in the province prior to applying for the divorce, then it may be rejected. The only solution in the long term is for more jurisdictions to expand the recognition of Canadian marriages for the purpose of divorce, whether the jurisdiction itself recognizes same-sex marriage.

SPERM DONATION

Fertility clinics use questionnaires to screen sperm donors. These questionnaires effectively block gay and bisexual men from donating sperm based on health and safety concerns about the statistically higher risk of HIV. However, this may even occur when the person wishing to receive the donation already knows the donor. The clinics do not appear at this time to take the sperm donation on a client-by-client basis, but instead rely on a general exclusion of that population. This has led to the use of "do it yourself" techniques in the gay and lesbian community and the use of sperm donor contracts between gay donor men and lesbian mothers. Are these contracts enforceable? That is unclear at this stage, but as we will see in the next section, same-sex families can get crowded.

SAME-SEX FAMILIES, ADOPTION, AND SPERM DONORS

If a lesbian couple uses a sperm donation and a child is born, who is legally entitled to call themselves a parent? Certainly, the biological mother and the biological father have legal status (if the sperm donor is identifiable). But does the non-biological lesbian partner of the biological mother also have parenting rights? If she does, is it possible for the child who was born to have three parents, all recognizable as having parental status? The answer is yes. As a result of a court decision in Ontario in 2006, it is possible for a lesbian couple and the sperm donor to form a three-parent family.

In some families the non-biological parent may wish to adopt the child that was born. However, because of our adoption laws, adoption can extinguish the parental rights of someone such as a sperm donor who may wish to remain involved with the child. These kinds of issues can be addressed in a sperm donation contract, particularly if the donor of the sperm wishes to stay involved in the child's life and perhaps even be considered a parent. It is an area of the law that involves a great deal of uncertainty at this time.

TRANSGENDERING

This issue has, to my knowledge, only arisen once, but concerned the impact of a sex reassignment by a parent on their entitlement to claim custody of or access to a child. In this particular case, a Canadian went through a sex reassignment process that would transform them from the male to the female sex. The female ex-partner of this individual argued in court that the sex reassignment undermined that former father's ability to act as a parent. The court examined the child's best interests and came to the conclusion that the parenting would not be affected by the sex reassignment. An unusual situation, but a cogent reminder that the court is really only concerned with the child's best interests when issues—even as unusual as this one—arise.

Issues concerning same-sex couples and Canadian family law continue to emerge. It is an area being followed closely by lawyers and the courts.

11

LET'S LOOK AT A MARRIAGE CONTRACT

In this chapter I have set out an entire draft marriage contract. Throughout the agreement I have inserted, from time to time, explanations about particular words or paragraphs to help you understand the purpose of that particular provision.

You will recall from Chapter 6, "Creating Your Own Set of Rights and Obligations," that as a couple you are free to include any terms you wish with respect to your property, spousal support, the day-to-day relationship, education and moral training of children, and any other matter related to your personal situation. However, you cannot include provisions that dictate custody of, and access to children, if and when they are born, or if and when you separate.

You will also recall that the court always reserves the right to disregard any provision not considered to be in the best interests of children. Similarly, any provision that tries to limit or eliminate an obligation to support a child will be disregarded by the court.

The following draft presents a sample agreement that includes some of the clauses that would be included in a basic agreement.

My annotations appear in italics. I hope a review of the draft and my comments help to promote questions and to focus your attention on clauses that might help you come to an agreement that suits both your needs.

MARRIAGE CONTRACT

It seems like a simple point, but it is important to name the document as a "Marriage Contract." This will prevent an argument at a later date that one of the parties to the agreement did not understand what he or she was signing. In at least one case, one of the spouses tried to characterize a promissory note and a mortgage as the equivalent of a marriage contract. The last thing you want to do is pay lawyers to fight over whether or not you actually signed a marriage contract.

THIS Marriage Contract made this ____________ day of ____________, 20___.

It is a small point, but you would be surprised how many people forget to put a date on the document. Unless you state otherwise somewhere in the agreement, such as on the signature page, this will be the date upon which the agreement comes into force.

B E T W E E N:

This part of the marriage contract is designed to set out who is entering into the agreement. It doesn't matter whose name appears first, but it does matter that you set out your correct legal names. A marriage contract is a contract and in this area you are setting out the parties to the contract.

____

(referred to as "____________")
and

____

(referred to as "____________")

WHEREAS:

Using the word "whereas" sounds a little legalistic, but it really is meant to say "this is the background to why we are entering into this contract." In these paragraphs you have an opportunity to set out details about the background of your relationship and matters that are of importance to why you are entering into the agreement. In this section you can include, for example, your ages, your birthdates, the names of children who are affected by the agreement, details of previous marriages and divorces, and, importantly, to say plainly what you are trying to achieve by having a marriage contract.

You will recall from Chapter 3, "Your Rights and Responsibilities to Each Other If You Are Married but Do Not Have a Marriage Contract," that it can be difficult to recall the actual moment of the beginning of your cohabitation. There is some significance to the date of marriage and the beginning of your cohabitation. In this subparagraph you have an opportunity to set out specifically the date upon which the marriage will occur or has occurred and, if you wish, the date upon which you began to cohabit, if you cohabited prior to getting married.

There was an interesting case in Nova Scotia in which a man and a woman separated after living together for about three years in a common-law relationship. This case concerns a common-law couple, but it still helps us to understand how to avoid confusion when entering into a marriage contract. The man had been hired on a six-month probationary contract to be the chief of a fire department and he needed to move to a new community and he did so, renting a fully furnished apartment while he waited to see if the probationary contract would become permanent.

Unfortunately, his common-law wife learned that he had been in a relationship with another woman and some discussions arose about whether she would join him even if the job became permanent. They sat down and negotiated a document in which he promised to pay to her $15,000 if and when he sold his home.

Later, his common-law wife refused to move to the new community and live with him and he contested his obligation to pay her

$15,000 upon the sale of home. He did so on the basis that there had been a misunderstanding about the circumstances under which $15,000 was to be paid. He thought he only had to pay if she moved with him.

This problem, which had to be litigated in a costly way in the courts, could have been avoided with some clearer paragraphs in the "whereas" section.

So when you are drafting your marriage contract take a few moments to write down exactly what it is you hope to achieve by the marriage contract and include those words in this section.

a) the parties intend to cohabit with one another commencing on __________ or have been cohabiting since _______________;

b) the parties intend this Marriage Contract to provide for their respective rights and obligations during separation or on death;

c) such rights and obligations (insert: *include ownership in or division of property, support obligations and the right to direct the educational and moral training of their children).*

NOW THEREFORE in consideration of the mutual covenants contained in this Agreement the parties agree as follows:

A marriage contract is a contract. In order to have a contract three things need to be present:

(1) Someone needs to offer to do something;

(2) Someone needs to accept the offer;

(3) There needs to be some consideration or thing of value that passes between the two parties to the contract in order to seal the bargain.

In some agreements parties will put "in consideration of the payment of One Dollar ($1) the parties agree as follows." In this particular draft marriage contract, the thing of value that is being exchanged between the parties—the consideration—are their promises and covenants to each other. I have never liked the idea of saying that a dollar seals the deal. I think the value of a marriage contract is the mutual promises the individuals are making to each other.

SEPARATION AGREEMENT WITH FORMER SPOUSE (IF THIS APPLIES)

If there are some previous obligations to a spouse and/or children, this should be set out early on in the marriage contract as a form of disclosure of existing commitments, and as recognition of both parties to the marriage contract that these obligations exist.

The paragraph above is very basic. In some cases it may be advisable to set out some of the important details of that separation agreement or even consider adding it as a schedule to the marriage contract. In that way there can be no misunderstanding about the disclosure by the party who has those existing rights and obligations.

1. __________ entered into a written Separation Agreement with his/her former spouse dated ________________, and has transferred all property and paid all sums required to be transferred or paid by him prior to the date of this Agreement.

OWNERSHIP AND DIVISION OF PROPERTY

Statement of Assets and Liabilities

2. The parties each have assets acquired prior to the date of this Agreement and although each party has had an opportunity to investigate, examine, and appraise the value of the assets of both parties and the quantum of the liabilities of both parties, neither party wishes to do so.

This clause is not intended to suggest that each party not investigate the assets and liabilities of their spouse. As was made clear in Chapter 9, financial disclosure is imperative to a strong marriage contract. The only time that such a clause might be applicable is in a situation where the couple has virtually nothing of value, but even that would only be known after disclosure has been made. The bottom line is this: do not try to simply rely on a paragraph such as this to alleviate the requirement for financial disclosure.

(a) _____________ represents that Schedule ___ contains a complete and accurate disclosure of all property registered in his/her name or of which he is the beneficial owner and of all debts whether presently owed or contingent.

b) _______________ represents that Schedule ____ contains a complete and accurate disclosure of all property registered in his/her name or of which she is the beneficial owner and of all debts whether presently owned or contingent.

You will recall from Chapter 6, "Creating Your Own Set of Rights and Obligations," that identification of assets that are not to be shared or assets that are being brought into the relationship is extremely important.

In the appendices, I have set out some work sheets and draft schedules to assist you in identifying and setting out your assets and liabilities as well as the value of those assets and liabilities. You will also recall from Chapter 9,"Signed, Sealed, and Delivered," the technical rules for making a marriage contract that will stand up, and that financial disclosure is critical to developing an enforceable contract. This disclosure is to be summarized in these schedules.

In every province and territory in Canada, legally married spouses have a statutory scheme for the division of their property in the event of separation and divorce. This is what makes them different from common-law couples. Common-law couples do not have a default statutory scheme. (For more information about common-law couples and cohabitation agreements, see my book Do We Need a Cohabitation Agreement?*)*

As discussed in Chapter 6: "Marriage Contracts: Creating Your Own Set of Rights and Responsibilities," when married couples enter into a marriage contract, they are in effect opting out of the statutory scheme that is provided by the provincial or territorial legislation. They are electing to create their own method of dividing property, providing for support, or dealing with issues concerning the education and moral upbringing of their children. Options for dividing property include: being separate as to property; designing their own community of property scheme; creating classes of property that are divided or not divided (e.g., family assets versus non-family assets). Alternatively, they may simply agree that the law of the province or territory applies to them with some specific exceptions.

In the following section, I have set out a scheme of property which focuses on creating a class of independent property—property that will not be shared in the event of separation or death. I am using this scheme as an example for this marriage contract. It is not the only way of designing a marriage contract; it is just an example.

Classes of Property to Remain Separate

3. The following property, which is referred to collectively as "Independent Property" shall be and remain the sole and exclusive property of the other party throughout the period the parties cohabit and in the event that they separate and upon the death of either party.

Note that this paragraph does two things:

(1) It sets out a category of property that will not be shared (referred to as "independent property."

(2) It also says that that category of property will be the sole and exclusive property of that particular party while the couple is together, if they separate, or if one of them dies.

The following paragraph sets out exceptions to the general rule that independent property will not be shared.

4. Subject to clause 1(c), neither party shall under any circumstances acquire any interest in "Independent Property":

(a) all real and personal property of the other party as described in Schedule "__" hereto;

You will recall from Chapter 6 that a common asset requiring protection through a marriage contract is a home owned by one of the spouses prior to the date of marriage. This situation arises when, for example, the husband-to-be acquired a home prior to marriage, one in which the couple intend to live after marriage. Without the benefit of a marriage contract, when that home is brought into the marriage, it enters the pool of assets to be divided. In other words, in the absence of a marriage contract, if the relationship breaks down, or the spouse dies, the value of that home will be divided even though it was acquired before the date of marriage. Spouses in this position often wish to protect that asset to ensure that it does not fall into the pool of assets that are divided. It will therefore be referenced in the Schedules attached to the marriage contract and it will also be referred to specifically in paragraph 13(e).

(b) all other real and personal property acquired by the other party prior to the date of this Agreement;

(c) all real and personal property acquired by the other party in his or her name alone and after the date of this Agreement;

(d) all income derived by the other party from any source;

(e) all gifts acquired by the other party from any source;

(f) all property received by the other party as damages; and

(g) all real and personal property inherited by the other party.

In this paragraph the parties are saying to each other that here are specific categories of property that we will not be sharing with each other:

(1) Property that is set out in Schedules A and B
(2) Property that was owned prior to the date of the agreement (which should be set out in the Schedules)
(3) Property that was purchased or acquired in a person's name alone after the date of the agreement. (in other words, RSPs or title to a property in that person's name alone)
(4) Any income they get from any source (this could be employment income, investment income, rental income)
(5) All gifts acquired from any source (this could include gifts from family members, friends, or business partners)
(6) Property received as damage. (this could include money that someone receives because they were in a car accident or injured on the job)

(7) Any property that is inherited by the person (this could be property that is inherited by virtue of a will or received because of an intestacy and the law dictates that they receive the property)

These are very broad categories of independent property and it amounts to saying "anything that is in my name now, or during the relationship is going to stay mine."

Exclusion of Interest as a Result of Operation of Law

This wording means that, as general as the foregoing exclusions are, here is a further clarification of how much is being excluded.

5. Without limiting the generality of the foregoing, neither party shall have the right to a division of any independent property, obtain an interest in any independent property, or shall have the right to compensation by reason of any direct or indirect contribution of the party not having an interest, whether by reason of :

(a) the use of the Independent Property;

If the couple uses independent property, on their own or as a family, it will not change the status of the property and the other spouse will not acquire an interest in that property. For example, if the family cottage is in the name of the husband, and the family uses it for many years, and the relationship then ends, the cottage will still be excluded from division.

(b) circumstances relating to the acquisition, disposition, preservation, or maintenance of the property;

You will recall the cases discussed in Chapter 4," The Legal Consequences of Marriage: Rights and Responsibilities If You Separate," In the absence of a marriage contract, all property acquired between the date of marriage and the date of separation will be placed in the asset pool for division. In some cases, individual spouses particularly value a piece of property because they invested money or labour and have a personal attachment to it. For example, consider the situation where a husband brought a family cottage into the relationship and the couple and their children ended up residing in the cottage for an extended period of time. If the wife spent time and labour improving the family cottage, there will likely be conflict between the husband and wife at the time of separation if the husband seeks an exemption of the cottage as an inherited property and the wife seeks an inclusion of it on the basis that she did extensive work and made an investment in its value. These types of problems can be avoided by stating clearly which properties are to be shared and which are not to be shared and by stating clearly that investment of money or labour in an excluded property will not change the fact that property will not be shared.

(c) maintenance or improvement of any Independent Property;

(d) the parties having disproportionate assets or liabilities; or

This clause makes it clear that the fact that one party has all the property and the other party has all the debt at the end of the relationship will not be a factor in giving a party an interest in property that is classified as independent.

(e) the assumption of responsibility for childcare, household management, or financial provision;

You will recall again the cases in which one spouse not only worked and contributed their wages to operation of the household budget, but also did all of the childcare and all of the household management. This clause is designed to make sure that each spouse understands that, if they choose to do those things, they will not be acquiring an interest in any of the property in the Independent Property category.

(f) any direct or indirect contribution of a party whether or not savings occur through effective management of the household or child rearing responsibilities;

To make it even clearer, this clause states that even if the work that was done or the contribution that was made by the spouse to the effective management of the household or the raising of the children resulted in the other spouse having a greater opportunity to work and build up his or her investment, this will not result in the spouse obtaining an interest in property classified as independent.

(g) the use of property for a family purpose;

Again, this clause makes it clear that, even if the family is using the property, it is not going to change its classification from that of Independent Property.

(h) any sacrifice made by a party including any sacrifice resulting in loss of career advancement or earning potential; or

This clause makes it abundantly clear that even if the spouse gave up opportunities in their career or passed up opportunities to earn more money, that decision is not going to result in them being compensated with an interest in Independent Property.

(i) any economic hardship that a party may suffer as a result of the relationship or its breakdown.

This clause is self-explanatory. It means that no matter how hard the breakdown of the relationship is, it is not going to result in an interest in this property.

Gifts and Dispositions Between the Parties

6. Nothing in this Agreement shall prevent either party from making gifts or testamentary dispositions to the other party.

This clause is designed to ensure that parties can give things to each other without worrying about which category they're going to fall into at a later point should the relationship end. A gift is a gift and it will remain that party's property should the relationship end. This clause also states that testamentary dispositions may be made. This means that spouses may leave gifts to each other in their wills. It also means that just because property was excluded for the purposes of the marriage, it does not block one spouse from giving the other spouse a gift.

For example, perhaps the family cottage is in the name of the husband alone and is classified as independent property. This marriage contract does not prevent the husband from leaving the family cottage to the wife in his will.

7. Notwithstanding the provision as to making gifts herein, the delivery of property of a value of over One Thousand Dollars ($1,000.00) from one party to the other will be deemed not to be a gift unless evidenced in writing and signed by the party making the gift.

The word "notwithstanding" creates a lot of confusion for people. It really means "even though I said something in the previous sentence, I want to say something more specific right now." The specific term that is being set out here is that "we won't keep track of gifts under $1,000, but if I give you a gift worth more than $1,000, it will need to be in writing and signed by me."

Division of Property on Separation or Death

8. Except as otherwise specifically provided in this Agreement, if the parties cease to cohabit for a period of 90 days or more or if one party dies, all property, real and personal, acquired during the period the parties cohabit which is not Independent Property shall be divided equally between the parties after having taken into account the income tax consequences of any transfer of interest and assets.

The effect of these few words is to say that if we split up for more than 90 days, or if one of us dies, property that doesn't fit into the Independent Property category is going to be divided equally. However, before its value is divided equally, income tax consequences are going to be taken into consideration. For example, if a husband owned a cottage in his name alone, but that cottage was not classified as Independent Property during the relationship and it needed to be transferred to the name of the wife, capital gains tax would be triggered and those taxes would be deducted from the value of the property to be shared equally between the two of them. In this way the income tax consequences of property that is owned equally is not the sole responsibility of just one person. The parties are going to be dividing the net value of their assets equally for assets that do fit in the category of Independent Property.

9. If the parties are unable to agree as to the actual division of the assets, either party may apply to a court of competent jurisdiction for an order allocating specific assets between the parties. If neither party applies for an allocation of assets to a court of competent jurisdiction and the parties are unable to agree on the allocation of assets, the assets shall then be sold and the net proceeds shall be divided equally between the parties forthwith. If the parties are unable to agree on the terms of the listing agreement or of the sale of the asset or assets, either party may apply to a court of competent jurisdiction for the determination of the dispute.

This means, if you can't agree, you are free to ask a court to make a division for you. If you do not want to go to court, but you still cannot agree on how to divide the particular assets, they will be sold and the net proceeds left after the sale will be divided equally between the two people.

If there is real estate involved and the couple needs to sign a listing agreement, but one person will not sign it, then you are off to court again for an order assisting with the sale of the property.

Tracing and Compensation for Benefits

10. If the parties cease to cohabit for a period of 90 days or more, or if one party dies and if either party has converted any Independent Property or any part thereof into other real or personal property that is not Independent Property, the following shall guide the division of property:

This is a very important provision in marriage contract. It allows a party who has Independent Property to trace that property into other assets. For example, if a party had excluded "all real and personal property inherited by the party" and had $100,000 in cash that they had inherited, and then took the $100,000 of Independent Property and purchased a piece of real estate that did not fit within the category of Independent Property, a method is provided to ensure that *the person who had the Independent Property receives a credit for the investment if and when the relationship ends.*

(a) Before the division referred to herein is effected, the value of the converted property (or the value of the part thereof) shall be traced into the other real or personal property;

Using the example of the $100,000 inheritance and the real property, the value of the inheritance would be traced into the value of the property that was acquired.

(b) The party who converted the property shall be reimbursed or given the value of the converted property (or the value of the part thereof);

The inheritance would be credited back to the person who purchased the real estate.

(c) The parties shall then share the net equity equally after deducting any liens, charges, or other encumbrances from the market value or sale price at the time.

Once credit has been given for the value of the traced inheritance, anything left over is then divided equally after deduction of liens, charges, or other encumbrances. So, if there is a mortgage on the property, or a contractor had registered a lien, those values are deducted after the inheritance value has been credited back to the other spouse. In this way, the spouse who owns Independent Property will always receive a credit should they move the value of their Independent Property around into various assets. Without this kind of provision, married couples with Independent Property would be forced to leave the property frozen in its original form if they wish to protect it.

(d) Provided that such tracing shall not occur where the party converting the property specifically elects in writing that the tracing shall not occur with respect to that particular property.

This provision allows the parties to agree that tracing will not occur for a particular piece of property, but note—it must be in writing. Verbal understandings will not be enough and won't be enforced.

SUPPORT

11. The parties acknowledge that they wish to remain completely independent of each other and each will be deemed to be self-supporting and not in need of support from the other. Each of the parties, at all times during the period of the marriage, or if they cease to cohabit, is responsible for supporting and maintaining himself or herself.

This is a blanket release of support but the wording is probably inadequate to ensure that the release would be enforced. It certainly captures the intentions of the parties in that it states that they wish to remain completely independent of each other financially, and that they are each self-supporting, but consider the following wording that appears in separation agreements and is considered to be a model clause for spousal support release at the time a couple separates.

Personally, I think that stronger language like the clause below is more likely to be upheld by a court if the parties truly wish to have blanket and complete releases of spousal support.

RELEASE OF SPOUSE SUPPORT

1. As a result of the terms of this agreement, the husband and the wife are financially independent of each other and release his or her rights to spousal support from the other forever. The husband and the wife intend this agreement to be forever final and non-variable.

2. The parties hereby acknowledge that:

(a) This agreement has been negotiated in an unimpeachable fashion and fully represents the intentions and expectations of the parties. Both parties have had independent legal advice and all the disclosure they have asked for and need in order to understand the nature and consequences of this agreement and come to the conclusion, as they do, that the terms of this agreement, including the release of all spousal support rights, constitutes an equitable sharing of both the economic consequences of their relationship and its breakdown.

(b) The provisions of this agreement take into account the overall objectives of Canadian Law now and in the future and, in particular, take into account the condition, means, needs, and other

circumstances of each spouse, including the length of time the parties have cohabited, the functions performed by each spouse during the cohabitation, and the other arrangements relating to the support of each spouse. The terms of this agreement substantially comply with the parties' need to exercise their autonomous rights to achieve certainty and finality.

(c) The terms of this agreement and, in particular this release of spousal support, reflect their own unique particular objectives and concerns. Among other considerations, they are also depending upon this spousal release, in particular, upon which to base their future lives.

3. The husband and the wife do not want the courts to undermine their autonomy as reflected in the terms of this agreement, which they intend to be a final and certain settling of all issues between them. They wish to be allowed to get on with their separate and independent lives, no matter what changes may occur. The husband and the wife specifically anticipate that one or both of them may lose their jobs, become ill and be unable to work, have childcare responsibilities that will interfere with their ability to work, find their financial resources diminished or exhausted whether through their own fault or not, or be affected by general economic and family conditions changing over time. Changes in their circumstances may be catastrophic, unanticipated, or beyond imagining. Nevertheless, no change, no matter how extreme, will alter this agreement and their view that the terms of this agreement reflect their intention to always be separate financially. The husband and the wife fully accept that no change whatsoever in their circumstances will entitle either of them to spousal support from the other.

4. The parties hereto specifically acknowledge and agree that they have specifically contemplated the provisions of s.15.3(3) of the Divorce Act and that the termination of spousal support is not related to the priority for spousal support for which provision is made pursuant to the aforesaid legislation.

12. Both parties accept the terms hereof in full satisfaction of all claims and causes of action which he or she now has or may hereafter acquire against the other for support.

Support Alternative for Household Expenses

The couple can divide responsibility for various expenses including such things as utilities, realty taxes, mortgage payments, credit card debt, or specific expenses related to the operation of the home. If one individual in the relationship wishes to lease a car, their lease payment could be confirmed as being their responsibility. If someone has a health club membership, it can be identified as a specific responsibility of one spouse.

13. Household and personal expenses shall be dealt with as follows:

(a) **Equal Sharing**

The parties shall share equally all costs relating to food, household goods, and furniture and appliance repair.

A list of expenses that are to be shared can be set out for complete clarification of obligations during the relationship.

(b) **Joint Bank Account**

The parties shall each pay their share of such costs into a joint bank account to be used by either of them for the purposes set out in this clause.

Some couples simply open a joint bank account and deposit their monthly agreed obligation to the account and then cover agreed-upon expenses out of that account by way of automatic deduction.

(c) **Living Expenses**

Each party shall pay for all other living expenses of himself or herself, including his or her own care expense, clothing costs, holiday expenses, as well as medical, dental, and prescription drug costs.

This clause clarifies each party's obligation for their own living expenses and complements paragraph 13 dealing with household expenses. For some couples, being specific is of great assistance to them to avoid arguing over budgets. It is also a valuable way of tracking each person's financial independence through the relationship.

(d) **Children**

_______ will be responsible for those expenses attributable to his/her children, namely:

Name of child: ________________ Date of birth: ___________

Name of child: ________________ Date of birth: ___________

Name of child: ________________ Date of birth: ___________

It may be a good idea also to acknowledge in this section another parent's support and where that support is allocated in the new family budget.

(e) **Home**

(i) **Ownership**: The lands and premises described in Schedule__, currently registered in the name of ____________ shall be used as the home of the parties (referred to as the "Home") but shall remain the exclusive Independent Property of ____________.

This provision is unequivocal confirmation that a home owned by the one spouse shall not be shared in the event of separation or death.

(ii) **Expenses**: All expenses relating to the Home including, without limiting the generality of the foregoing, the financial encumbrances, taxes, upkeep, and maintenance of the Home shall be paid by ______________.

"Without limiting the generality of the foregoing" means that some examples are about to be given, but the examples in no way are exhaustive.

A unique entitlement for legally married spouses is the right to claim possession of the matrimonial home. As discussed in Chapter 6, legally married spouses have special rights and obligations with respect to matrimonial homes. For example, as we have seen, a property owned by one spouse prior to the marriage that is brought into the marriage and used as a matrimonial home, loses any special protection and falls into the family asset pool for division. This occurs unless a marriage contract provides otherwise. So, it is possible in a marriage contract to protect the title to a piece of property that is used as a matrimonial home.

However, even though a spouse may give up the right to make a claim against the value of a matrimonial home, they cannot give up the right to claim possession of the matrimonial home at the time the relationship breaks down. This protection was placed in provincial and territorial family law to ensure that a spouse who had given up an interest in the value of property was not thrown on the street. Imagine, for example, a situation in which a relationship broke down because of domestic violence. This protection allows the spouse who was perhaps a victim of the domestic violence to claim the right to possession of the home for a period of time even though they may ultimately have no financial interest in that property.

This right to claim possession of the matrimonial home, regardless of ownership, cannot be given up in a marriage contract. However, it is possible to provide some guidance for how notice to vacate could be given in a situation where the relationship has broken down, the home is owned by one spouse, and there is a need to ease the spouse who has no interest in the home out and into their own new residence. The following paragraphs set out an approach to giving notice to vacate. It is possible to include these provisions on the understanding that the ability of the court to order that a spouse receive possession at the time of breakdown could very well override it.

(iii) **Notice to Vacate:** ___________ may give ___________ 30 days' notice to vacate the Home, after which period ___________ shall leave ___________ in sole and exclusive occupancy of the Home.

This provision allows the owner of the home to give notice to the other spouse if the relationship comes to an end. In addition, it would allow an executor or estate trustee of the estate of a deceased person to give notice to a spouse who continued to reside in the home.

(iv) During the period that ___________ resides in the Home after___________ has given the notice and up to the time that he/she vacates the Home, ___________shall not entertain anyone in the Home nor shall he/she change the Home in any way.

This provision is necessary because it could be unpleasant to have the spouse who is moving out entertaining in the home during the 30-day period or making changes to the home in that 30-day period. It is also possible, of course, to add some wording to this clause that would allow for extensions of the 30-day period by the owner of the property. It is not always possible for someone to find alternative accommodations in a 30-day period.

(f) **Estates**

Subject to the provisions of this Agreement, neither party shall claim any interest in the estate of the other except as specifically provided for by Will or, in the case of an intestacy, as specifically provided for by the laws of the governing jurisdiction relating to the intestate succession.

See also Chapter 5: "The Legal Consequences of Marrying: Rights and Responsibilities If One of You Die, or Is Injured." All provinces allow a surviving spouse to claim support from the estate if they were indeed dependent upon the deceased person at the time of their death. In addition, provincial and territorial law provides a surviving legally married spouse with the ability to claim an interest in property of the deceased spouse. This is a right that distinguishes legally married couples from common-law couples in most provinces. This provision is designed to block any claim of a surviving spouse unless some provision is contained in the marriage contract or the will entitling them to property or support.

(g) **Testamentary Provisions**

The parties have each made valid Wills naming the other as beneficiary to the extent of $______ and agree not to change their Wills. This provision shall always be a first charge on the Estate of the deceased party.

It is possible for legally married spouses to make what are known as "mutual wills." They can also enter into an agreement requiring them not to change their wills after it has been signed. In some cases an actual contract is signed confirming that agreement. Courts have been willing to enforce mutual wills if there is adequate evidence that the parties had indeed agreed to do so. If a party changes his or her will and therefore violates the agreement, the court may ignore the new will and enforce the previous will against the estate.

This provision allows the surviving spouse who relied upon an agreement for mutual wills to enforce that agreement against the estate of the deceased spouse. In this regard see also paragraph (m) of the marriage contract (below) which makes the marriage contract binding on the heirs, executors, and administrators of a deceased spouse's estate.

(h) **Care of Children of Former Unions**

(i) **Children**: The following children of ______________ and his former relationship shall reside with the parties:

Name of child: ______________ Date of birth: ______________
Name of child: ______________ Date of birth: ______________
Name of child: ______________ Date of birth: ______________

It may be a good idea to set out the actual anticipated residential schedule for the children so that there is no misunderstanding about the potential obligations, including not just day-to-day schedules but schooling commitments, major holidays, and summer vacations.

(ii) **Expenses**: All expenses related to the said children, including all expenses for their care and upbringing, shall be the sole responsibility of ______________.

(iii) **Compensation for services**: Where ______________ provides household or childcare services for such children, he/she shall receive reasonable compensation from ______________ for such services within 14 days of the end of the month in which such services were provided. If such compensation is not received, he/she shall receive such compensation within 14 days of delivery of a written calculation of the value of such services to______________.

This provision is optional. It is unnecessary to provide for such compensation given the provisions of paragraph. 2(c)(iv). However, if compensation for childcare or household services seems appropriate in your particular relationship, this is a useful clause.

(iv) If there is a dispute as to the amount of compensation as shown in the written calculation, ____________ shall arbitrate the dispute, and such decision shall be binding upon both parties.

(v) If no written calculation and request for compensation is delivered within the 14-day time period stipulated above, there shall be no claim in the future for household or childcare services performed.

(j) **Documents**
Without limiting the generality of the foregoing, each party shall do all things necessary to facilitate the fulfillment of the terms of this Agreement by both parties including, providing further information and executing further documents.

This provision is necessary because, at some point in the future, it may be important to have a spouse sign important documents to give effect to the agreement. For example, signing of a listing agreement for a property, signing mortgage documents or transfer documents, tax returns or tax designations related to capital gains, and so on.

(j) **Entire Agreement**
This Agreement constitutes the entire agreement between the parties and supersedes all previous communications, representations, and agreements, whether verbal or written, between the parties with respect to the subject matter hereof.

This is a very important clause. It confirms that the only agreement is the agreement that is in writing. If the couple has verbal discussions or if they write notes to each other, that type of information will not change the interpretation of the marriage contract. The only changes that will be valid are changes that are made in exactly the same way that the agreement was made in the first place—written, signed, and witnessed. In this regard see paragraph (n) below.

(k) **Severability**
The invalidity of any particular clause or subclause of this Agreement shall not affect any other clause or subclause of this Agreement, but this Agreement shall be construed as if such invalid clause or subclause were omitted.

This clause allows the marriage contract to be scrutinized and should one clause be considered invalid, it will not wipe out the legal effect of the balance of the agreement. For example, if a couple included a provision that a court considered to affect custody of or access to children, or a provision that eliminated an entitlement to child support, that type of clause could be struck from the marriage contract without affecting the balance of it.

(l) **Applicable Law**

This Agreement is made pursuant to the laws of ____________. It shall be interpreted pursuant to the laws of____________ and the jurisdiction for any adjudication related to this Agreement shall be the ____________ Court (e.g., *The parties intend this Agreement to be a Marriage Contract in accordance with the provisions of the* Family Law Act, R.S.O. 1990, c.F.3 , *as amended from time to time*).

This provision allows you to select the law of a particular province or territory to govern the interpretation of your marriage contract. Even if the couple resides in Manitoba, for example, they could select the law of Ontario to govern their marriage contract.

(m) **Heirs and Executors**

This Agreement shall also be binding upon the heirs, executors, and administrators of the parties to this Agreement, who shall do all things necessary for the purpose of carrying out the terms of this Agreement as may then be applicable.

As you will recall from Chapter 5, legally married spouses have specific entitlements to make claims against the estate of a deceased partner. Unlike common-law spouses in most provinces, legally married spouses have statutory entitlements to claim property from the estate or to elect to be treated as if they had separated the day before their spouse died. This paragraph confirms that the heirs, executors, estate trustees, and even administrators in the case of an intestacy are bound by the contents of the marriage contract. This means, for example, that Independent Property as set out in the marriage contract will be preserved and will fall into the deceased spouse's estate, that property will be protected in the same way in which it would have been protected had the couple simply separated.

(n) **Amendments**

This Agreement may be amended only by written agreement between the parties with such agreement made in the same way that this Marriage Contract has been made, in writing, signed, and witnessed.

Remember, handwritten notes and verbal understandings are not going to be enforceable. If the agreement needs to be amended, it must be amended in the same way that it was created. It must be in writing, signed, and witnessed. It does not need to be witnessed by the same individuals who witnessed the original marriage contract.

(o) **Legal Advice, Disclosure, and Fair Agreement**

Each of the parties acknowledges that he or she:

(i) has had independent legal advice (insert: as evidenced by the execution of the certificates attached to this agreement);

If one party is not receiving independent legal advice, see the acknowledgment that is at the end of this agreement, whereby a person can acknowledge that they had an opportunity to obtain independent legal advice, but decided not to.

(ii) understands the nature and consequences of this Agreement;

See Chapter 9, "Signed, Sealed, and Delivered" with its stress on the importance of ensuring that both parties understand exactly what the agreement is attempting to achieve and its effect, both as of the date it is signed and possible implications for the future. Avoid "kitchen table agreements" where you witness each other's signatures. The court will be reluctant to enforce such agreements. It is not worth the risk. Find someone to witness your signatures and you will increase the likelihood of enforceability.

(iii) is signing this Agreement voluntarily;

See also Chapter 9, in particular, those passages on the importance of ensuring that a party is not under duress or undue influence when they sign the agreement.

(iv) has made full disclosure to the other of his or her respective significant assets, debts, and liabilities existing at the date of this Agreement as evidenced by the statements contained in Schedules; and

See also Chapter 9 with reference to the importance of making full financial disclosure, both in terms of assets, debts, and liabilities and the value or extent of those assets, debts, and liabilities.

(v) believe that the provisions of this Agreement adequately discharge the present and future responsibilities of the parties to one another and that the contract will not result in circumstances that are unconscionable or unfair to either party (alternate: believes that the provisions of this Agreement are fair).

You will recall that in some cases the court may be prepared to interfere with a marriage contract if the effect of it is unconscionable. This subparagraph is an acknowledgment that the parties consider the agreement to be fair and specifically state that it is not unconscionable or unfair to either of them.

IN WITNESS WHEREOF the parties have hereunto signed their names the day and year first above written:

______________________	______________________
Witness	By
______________________	
Name	
______________________	
Address	
______________________	
Occupation	

See also Chapter 9, in particular the proper way to have these agreements witnessed. It is important to have the witness present at the time the agreement is signed by the party whose signature they are purporting to witness.

CERTIFICATE OF INDEPENDENT LEGAL ADVICE

See Chapters 8 and 9 to understand the significance of obtaining not only independent legal advice, but effective independent legal advice.

I,_______________, of the ______________ , in the_______________ , Barrister and Solicitor, hereby certify that:

1. I was consulted in my professional capacity by_______________, one of the parties named in the annexed Marriage Contract dated as of _____________, as to his/her rights and obligations under the said Agreement.

2. I acted solely for him/her and explained to him/her the nature and effect of the said Marriage Contract, and he/she acknowledged and declared that he/she fully understood the provisions thereof and it appeared to me that he/she was executing the said Marriage Contract of his/her own volition and without fear, threat, compulsion, or influence by _______________ or any other person.

3. I am subscribing witness to the said Marriage Contract, and I was present and saw it executed by_____________ at _____________ on __________ .

DATED at___________ this___________ day of___________, 20___.

____

Name of Solicitor

This acknowledgment below can be modified to reflect your actual circumstances. The effect of this acknowledgment is to ensure that a party who has not obtained independent legal advice acknowledges that they had an opportunity to do so. The person who witnesses the signature related to this acknowledgment should be careful to review each paragraph in the acknowledgment with the person who is signing it. In this way it will reduce the likelihood of that acknowledgment being attacked at a later date as having been signed under duress or undue influence.

ACKNOWLEDGMENT OF....................

1. I, ________________, one of the parties to a Marriage Contract dated the _____day of_____________, 20_, acknowledge that I was advised by______________ that he/she could not act for both parties to this Marriage Contract, that he/she represents only my spouse, and that I should seek and obtain independent legal advice before signing this Marriage Contract.

2. Notwithstanding the above, I choose not to seek independent legal advice, and to sign this Marriage Contract not having had the benefit of such advice.

3. I do hereby further declare and acknowledge that:

(a) The said ______________ has not purported to advise me with respect to my rights and obligations under this Marriage Contract;

(b) I have carefully read the provisions of the Marriage Contract and understand the meaning of each and every one of them;

(c) I have signed the Marriage Contract of my own volition, without the pressure of undue influence or coercion of any kind on the part of my spouse or his/her lawyer; and

(d) I do verily believe that the provisions of the Marriage Contract are fair, reasonable, and adequate to protect my interests and those of my spouse.

IN WITNESS WHEREOF I have hereunto signed my name this day of____________, 20___.

SIGNED
in the presence of:

______________________	______________________
Witness	By

____

Name

~

The foregoing draft marriage contract is designed to assist you in gathering your own thoughts about the possible contents for a marriage contract. Do not hesitate to work with this draft and perhaps consider obtaining some independent legal advice from a lawyer about the way in which the agreement is evolving. You will recall from Chapter 8 that it may not be necessary to hire a lawyer for completion of the agreement from start to finish. It is possible to simply buy an hour or two of advice from time to time to make sure you're on the right track.

Appendices

Appendix A

MY MARRIAGE CONTRACT WORKSHEET—WHAT I OWN AND WHAT I OWE

What do I own?	What is it worth?
1. Real estate	
2. Cottage/recreational property	
3. Vehicles	
4. RRSPs/Savings	
5. Pensions	
6. Stocks and investments	
7. Companies/sole proprietorships	
8. Timeshares	
9. Accounts receivable	
10. Jewellery	
11. Art	
12. Memberships	
13. Sporting equipment	
14. Musical instruments	
15. Furniture	
16. Other property	

What do I owe?	How much and for how long?
1. Mortgages	
2. Line of credit	
3. Credit cards	
4. Taxes	
5. Loans from family	
6. Other loans	
7. Lawsuits	
8. Judgments	
9. Fines	

Appendix B

MARRIAGE CONTRACT SCHEDULE A AND SCHEDULE B

SCHEDULE A
My Marriage Contract Asset and Liability Summary

Asset	Value

Liability	Amount of Liability

SCHEDULE B
My Marriage Contract Asset and Liability Summary

Asset	Value

Liability	Amount of Liability

Appendix C

SOME CONSIDERATIONS AND KEY DOCUMENT CHECKLIST

A. CONCERNS ABOUT CHILDREN

- Will we have children? Our own? Adoption? How many?
- When would we have children?
- Would one of us stay home from our career?
- What are our attitudes about child rearing?
- What do we each think about religious upbringing?
- Education? Public? Private? Religious?
- Health care? Benefits available?
- Recreation/Sports/Hobbies/Clubs?
- Sunset/Termination clauses needed?

B. CONCERNS ABOUT FINANCES

- What are our attitudes about finances?
- What are our debt/assets situations?
- Future liabilities/current savings?
- Taxes owed?
- Future career plans—1 year? 5 years? 10 years?
- Will we buy property? How acquired? Joint account?
- Rent? How will we pay?

- Inheritances now? In future?
- Life insurance?
- Disability insurance?
- Pensions?
- Obligations to previous spouse and children. How much? How long?
- Wills, powers of attorney, letters of intent on joint accounts?

C. CONCERNS ABOUT HEALTH

- Significant medical history?
- Family history? Risk? What if one of us gets sick?
- Health risk through employment?
- Mental health history? Concerns?
- Alcohol?
- Drugs?
- Gambling?
- Obsessive-compulsive disorder?
- Schizophrenia? Bipolar? Manic Depressive?
- Criminal convictions? Pending issues? Record? Pardon?
- Wills, Power of Attorney for Personal Care?

D. CONCERNS ABOUT PROPERTY

- How acquired? Contributions?
- How would title be held? Joint? Sole? Tenants-in-common?
- Family property? Inherited?
- Business assets? Inherited? Incorporated?
- Business partners? Working together?
- Maintenance and improvement of each other's property?
- Wills, Power of Attorney for Property?
- When did our cohabitation begin?

DO I HAVE . . .

A Will?

Where is it?
Who is my executor/estate trustee?
Does it need updating?

A Power of Attorney for Personal Care?

Where is it?
Who is the attorney?
Who is the alternate?
Does it need updating?
Does it contemplate instructions for care in the case of emergencies?

A Power of Attorney for Property?

Where is it?
Who is the attorney?
Who is the alternate?
Does it need updating?

Joint Assets/Accounts?

If real estate, where are the documents?
If accounts, what are the account numbers and institutions?
What is our intention with respect to joint assets?
Do I have a letter of intent for joint accounts? Where is it?

Appendix D

CONSENT FOR DISCLOSURE OF CRIMINAL HISTORY INFORMATION

I, ____

Given Name Middle Name Surname

(Other Surnames) ______________________________________

Gender. Male Female

Born on the __________ day of ____________, 20____

Address: ______________________________________

____

____

having voluntarily provided the above noted personal information, hereby authorize any Canadian Police Agency to conduct a CPIC (Canadian Police Information Centre) search of the "National Repository for Criminal Records in Canada," and any other police information system to which they have access, for criminal information history pertaining to me, for the purpose of obtaining employment, other than employment that involves working with children or other vulnerable persons. I am aware that this search does not include criminal convictions for which a pardon has been granted, nor does it include criminal offences that fall under the Youth Criminal Justice Act (YCJA). Therefore, at this time and until I specifically inform you to the contrary in writing, in compliance with all Municipal, Provincial, and Federal human rights and privacy legislation, I hereby authorize that the results of this search be released to International Fingerprinting Services Canada (IFSC), who will provide the results directly to:

____

____

____

Signature of Applicant______________________________

Date____________________

Appendix E

PERMISSION TO CONDUCT CREDIT REFERENCES

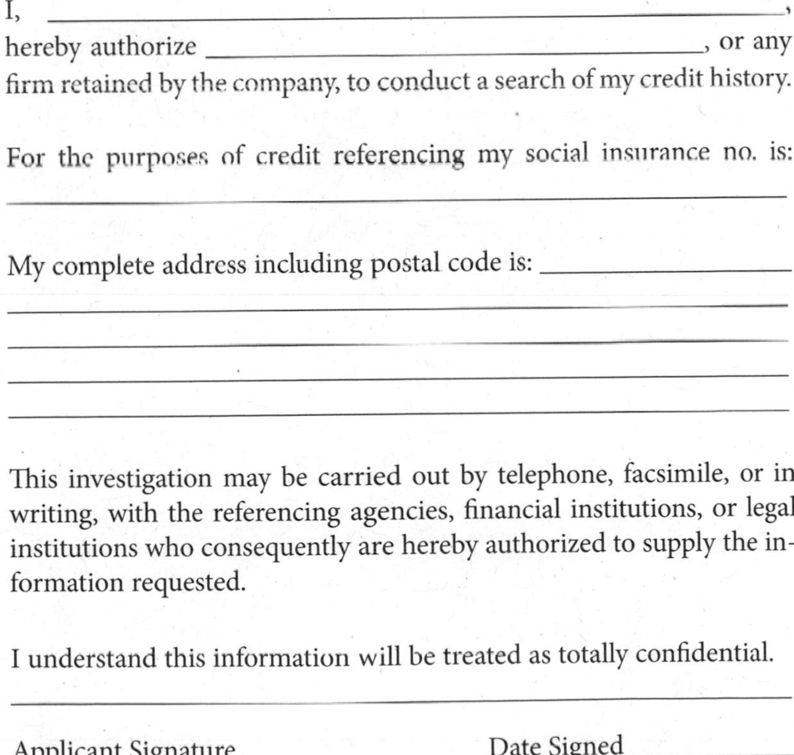

I, ____,
hereby authorize ______________________________, or any firm retained by the company, to conduct a search of my credit history.

For the purposes of credit referencing my social insurance no. is:
____

My complete address including postal code is: ________________
____
____
____
____

This investigation may be carried out by telephone, facsimile, or in writing, with the referencing agencies, financial institutions, or legal institutions who consequently are hereby authorized to supply the information requested.

I understand this information will be treated as totally confidential.

____

Applicant Signature________________ Date Signed ____________

INDEX

D

E

F

G

H

I

J

K

L

Q

R

S

MAKE YOUR NOTES HERE

MAKE YOUR NOTES HERE

MAKE YOUR NOTES HERE

MAKE YOUR NOTES HERE

MAKE YOUR NOTES HERE

MAKE YOUR NOTES HERE